Book of Spells

THE ART OF MASTERING
INCORRUPTIBLE MAGIC

ALMINE

Published by Spiritual Journeys LLC

Copyright October 2014

P.O. Box 300
Newport, Oregon 97365

US toll-free number: 1-877 552 5646

www.spiritualjourneys.com

Cover Illustration – Charles Frizell

ISBN 978-1-936926-70-1 Hardcover

Table of Contents

WWW.IAMPRESENCE.COM/SPELLS

Foreword

All fairy spells' commentary is given in their exact and sometimes childlike words.

Interdimensional photography distorts the clarity of the outlines of form since form is more fluid in other dimensions than in physical life. The colors appear more red, orange or yellow depending on the dimension.

For a video clip showing the fairies around one of the Seer Almine's support team, see: www.iampresence.com/spells/fairy-video

The Blahut Sigil — Power Source of Angel Magic

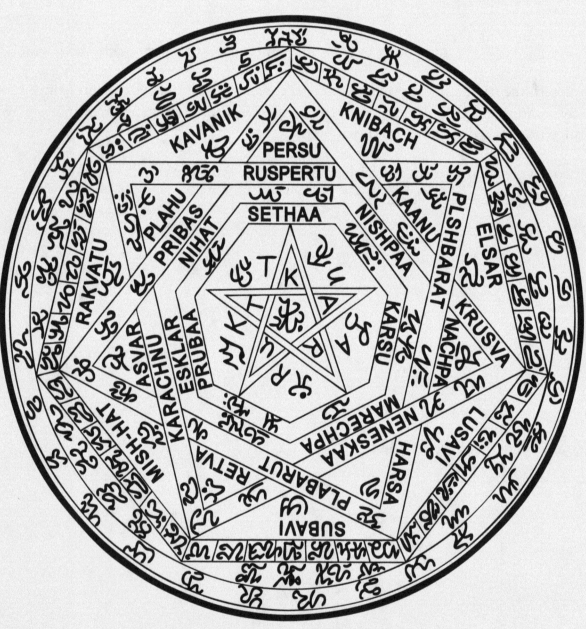

The Blahut Sigil is the advanced Sigil for Angel Magic
and is used for these spells. It is also the center of the Power Wheel of Merging Realities.

The Wheel of Merging Realities

Introduction to Incorruptible Magic

What is Magic?

First Ring versus Second Ring Magic

In speaking of the magic kingdoms, it is necessary to lift the veil from magic and its uses. Magic is the manipulation of reality through the use of intent. There are two ways to practice magic: first ring magic and second ring magic.

On the walls of ancient Central American ruins, the story is told of how first ring magic was initially brought to Earth by star beings from Orion. This form of magic is left-brain based and utilizes external techniques for its effectiveness. When most speak or think of magic, it is usually first ring magic to which they refer.

Second ring magic uses right-brain, feminine, non-cognitive methods of affecting reality. The magic originates from within rather than from without. It is inner abilities that are used by the unseen realms on Earth.

Among the kingdoms and realms on Earth, only the physical ones have forgotten their heritage as magical beings of the cosmos. As a result, their ability to do second ring magic became obscured and man resorted to left-brain or first ring magic.

Only in the deepest recesses of the mystery schools did pockets of knowledge survive of an inner technology that could influence the environment in mystical ways. Only there were remnants taught of the knowledge that once flourished in ancient Mu and some of the older Atlantean civilizations.

The advent of first ring magic wrought havoc among men. Climates were disrupted, global catastrophes occurred and men became power-seekers and turned upon each other. The oral traditions of the Toltec seers speak of these times of great destruction when first ring magic was used in warfare that destroyed and ravaged Atlantis.

Between 200,000 and 75,000 years ago, when Atlantis was divided into two large islands, Ruta and Itiya, practitioners of first ring magic congregated on Ruta and grew strong.

Those practicing second ring magic lived on Itiya, laboring diligently to keep the Earth from experiencing another global catastrophe. At the end of the period however, it became abundantly clear they were losing the battle. They fled to safer areas, including the inner Earth.

The only way to obtain power without damaging the interconnectedness of life is through perception. First ring magic used ritual, incantations and other external sources of power. This must eventually deplete not only the practitioner, but the environment. In addition, the power available through left-brain methods is limited, whereas that available through the right-brain, internal methods is not.

First ring magic causes environmental disruption and catastrophe through depleting the environment and disrupting the Earth's energetic flow. The planetary energy flows along its ley lines or meridians. In addition, each species has a grid telling it how to act. These grids are arrays of lines along which light, in the form of information, flows. When these, as well as the ley lines, are disrupted, the planet tilts on her axis or draws in other catastrophes due to a lack of life force. The potential for abuse of magic is a very real threat when first ring magic is used, since it doesn't require that the practitioner develop impeccability. Knowledge of certain practices is all that is needed. Power seekers have disrupted the environment with first ring magic since its introduction to humanity.

Second ring magic, on the other hand, is the result of perception. In fact, the more inclusive the perception, the more power is available. Practitioners, because of their increased perception, become unable to harm life.

For the most part, the magical kingdoms have very strict rules governing the use of magic, with dire consequences for its misuse. Exceptions have been, among others, the demons and sometimes the dragons. Since the planetary and cosmic ascension began, the Mother Goddess has decreed that power to do magic be matched by a corresponding degree of perception. This removed the destructive magical abilities from beings in the cosmos.

Second ring magic has been used by fairies, elves, pixies and other beings from the magical kingdoms to create, grow and sustain plant and mineral life. Angels have done the same for human and animal life. Large planetary angels sustain planets; smaller ones govern oceans, rivers, lakes and mountain ranges. Angels support humans in many ways, some staying with a single human all his life, much as a guardian spirit would. Therefore it can be said that magic, or the power of intent, is the primary force that carries out the will of the Infinite within the cosmos. Only when it becomes exclusive or self-centered does it destroy rather than sustain life.

The Andromedan Fairy

So small are the Andromedan fairies that angels had to carry them to Earth, or it would have taken them 300 years to reach us. Compare their size to photos previously taken of other fairies.

An Andromedan fairy flutters in front of Seer Almine during the candle-light ceremony.

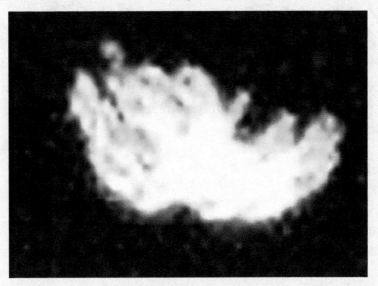

Close-up of Andromedan fairy.

Close-up of a different fairy fixing the grass.

The Fairy Song:
Arlu Praveesh Parhem

On the night of November 8th, 2006, a little male fairy came to my house to give me a song called Arlu Praveesh ("ee" sound as in "eat") Parhem. I asked him the following questions.

Q. What is your name?
A. Green.

Q. Can you tell me about the song?
A. Your words are hard, hard.

Q. Do you mean it's hard to communicate with me?
A. Yes, hard, hard, hard.

Q. Is the song in preparation for the Fairy Magic hat is soon to come from the fairies from Lyra?
A. Yes, yes, yes. It is so exciting!
(Just then my phone rang and he asked if he could wait on my back porch. I said yes, I would call him after my conversation.)

Q. What does this song do? Is it to unlock the flow of information?
A. It is a mystery, mystery, mystery.

Q. You mean I have to wait before understanding it till it's the right moment?
A. Yes. This is so exciting!

Q. I am excited too. Thank you. Am I doing it right? (The song was not in any scale that I was familiar with.)
A. Yes, yes, yes.

On November 13th, the thousands of fairies from Lyra who gathered here on earth, shared their magic spells with us. It was then that I realized the purpose of this little song: it removed the protective shield that surrounds the incantations, so that I would be able to hear them.

Arlu Praveesh Parhem

The Pronunciation of the Fairy Language

For those who speak a Germanic language, the pronunciation is easier. It is as though you are reading German, with the exception of the "v". The syllables are pronounced with equal value: "Ba-ravek," for example, has equal emphasis on every syllable.

Pronunciation:

a – as in pardon

e – as in beckon

o – as in border

u – as in true

ch – as in the German, "buch" (or "kh")

ee – as in please

aa – as in spa

v – as in Victor

sh – as in ship

w – as in wide

They don't use percentages; the percentage is seen in the mind as a partial apple or other object like a pie. The fairy language has no past or future tense, since only the moment exists.

Third Ring of Magic and the Evolution of Power

The Evolution of Power

The world around us can only be changed without karmic repercussions if we change it indirectly. If we try and change it directly, we are trying to force our will onto the ever-changing flow of existence. This is, in the broadest sense, a form of black magic – no matter how well intended we are. There are two types of karmic chains we can wear: The iron chains of hurtful deeds and the golden chains of good deeds. Good deeds stem from the arrogance of thinking that we can fix life.

Trying to directly change your circumstances is often not very successful. One who tries to master lucid dreaming knows that when you try to study an object directly in the dream, you are immediately pulled into another part of the dream. The dream changes as a result of direct focus. The outcome of scientific experiments change depending on which scientist is doing the experiment. Therefore, trying to change something that alters when you focus on it is not effective.

There are two approaches to change the environment:

1. To capture circumstances and enforce changes on it using an external power source. This is called first ring magic or black magic. It creates karmic repercussions because it dams up the flow of life, and because all of life is interconnected, causes stress and pain (forced change) somewhere in life.

2. The indirect approach allows life to unfold, but eliminates those factors that cause obstruction, through emphasizing something else. The shift of emphasis changes the outcome indirectly. This is second ring magic.

Personal power decreases when we try and force our will (resistance) onto life, and when we become dependent on external power sources such as various allies. Personal power increases through the use of second ring magic, or the indirect principles of manifestation.

Changing the world to a reality of more graceful unfolding has been a quest of lightworkers. Yet many have shunned the study of how to achieve the power necessary for a beneficial contribution. Power has been feared as something that can pollute their purity, and thus it has been left in the hands of the ill-intended. Mastering the impeccable use of personal power is essential for those who wish to contribute to a better world.

There are three different ways of affecting reality indirectly:

1. Through the use of Perception (Transfiguration)

Perception yields power – something light seekers will encounter whether they are prepared for it or not. The power can be directed through intent, but we will then run the risk of imposing our will on life.

Perception based tools such as rituals, runes, incantations and healing modalities like Belvaspata can indirectly broadcast intent when accompanied by insights. The focus is on the insight, deflecting it from a specified outcome. A broad intention is set such as: "I enter into the full abundance of my being." The specifics of how the money and other resources will come, is not focused on.

As the perception removes obstructed vision, the power tied up in keeping obstructions in place is released and directed into the ceremony or ritual which has been set up for the purpose of broadcasting your broad intention. This mobilizes elements to manifest your hopes in a far more spectacular way than you could have visualized yourself. All you have to do is hold an attitude of glad expectation.

2. Through the use of Frequency and Resonance (Transmutation)

The use of frequency and resonance to powerfully affect our environment uses emphasis to increase the desirable elements in our surroundings. If we wish to have more abundance, we begin by being more abundant with ourselves in terms of time to relax, fulfilling the little desires of our heart, etc. If we wish to be loved and accepted, we stop abandoning ourselves in favor of others.

When difficult people are in our lives, we find within them the praiseworthy part that we can resonate with and emphasize it as a song in our heart when we are with them. We look past the difficult exterior and feel their resonant aspects vibrate with ours in perfect harmony.

3. Through removing Obstructive Filters (Transformation)

We remove the obstruction in our environment by finding a similar obstructiveness within ourselves, and removing it through insight and intent. We honor the purpose served by the filter in our vision or the obstructive attitude, but recognize that it is time for a higher vision. In this way we avoid the pitfall of strengthening what we oppose.

The Third Ring of Magic

The word magic has been misused for centuries. It never was intended to mean the ability to impose one's will on life. Magic, in its true meaning, means to expose the Infinite perfection and design of unfolding existence. In third ring magic, you become so at one with the Infinite's will, that you know there is nothing to change. You are able to contribute to the quality of the endless journey. Like a treasure hunt, the journey yields joyous discoveries of the eternal self hidden within the many. Knowing this, is to appreciate all life as an extension of the self. When this point is reached, the inner knowing that all you can ever change is yourself becomes certain.

12

Gifts from the Magical Kingdoms

WHITE MAGIC FROM THE HIDDEN REALMS

A rose fairy sits camouflaged in a rose.

Magic from the Fairy Realms

How to Cultivate Magic From the Fairies behind Niagara Falls

A TABLET FROM THE STONE BOOKS LIBRARY
IN THE PIENINY MOUNTAINS, POLAND
THE MESSAGE OF STONE BOOK I

Behind the waterfall [1] under the stone
Waits a book of how to do magic for pure eyes alone
Enter with laughter and you may remain
But return to your childhood yet again
With the heart of a child you were given before [2]

1. Niagara Falls
2. Humans received magical codes in 2007.

The Tuning Fork Tree

Photo taken by Helena, Canada

The 24 Fairy Secrets of Relearning How to Do White Magic

1. Find a singing tree and hear its tones. Sit in silence against its trunk. Listen to the song, though not with your ears. When you hear it, your cells will start to dance. When you do this often, the magic will come.

The Greeting the Fairies Use for a Tree

Piki Pa Pahu

Note: They recommend trees that look like tuning forks.

2. Walk barefoot in the dew to clear neural pathways.[3] The reflexology points on the bottom of the feet are affected by the dew. (I asked them how.) "The dew drops tickle the blades of grass and their laughter ripples through the dew. That's why dew is so special. It's good for cuts too, so the injured area can feel good again."

3. Create a fairy circle and say these words:

Paalik biliblat hispiva nesut.

Make it of flowers, shells and the feathers of birds. Sit in it and listen when the moon is full. Hear our bells and songs we'll sing for you.

4. Learn to listen with your skin. Feel the vibrations like music within. Feel the notes stroke you and listen within. The use of omnipresent senses is where magic begins.

5. Practice refining your sense of smell. Then the energy[4] will rise up the spine as well. The codes of magic in the spine lie. Thus smell awakens the energy that at the base of the spine hides.

6. Find a clear stream and on its bank lie. Listen to it talk as you close your eyes. Not with its voice does it talk to you, but imagine the stream is flowing through you. See where it's been as it flowed on its way. Become the stream to know what it'll say.

---

3. Old Swiss folk remedies also suggest this.
4. Kundalini

7. As the hawk, so too you can fly, effortlessly soaring through the sky. Become the hawk; let your spirit be free. Practice it often until you can feel the wind through your feathers, until the Earth below you can see.

8. Magic is through joy and abundant delight, strengthened within the cord of the spine. Make a list of what brings you pleasure; incorporate it in your life to the fullest measure. Incorporate the giving of joy to yourself each day that you live, for the rest of your life.

9. To bring joy to others creates a flow that strengthens your magic. This you must know. Find ways to surprise them, let your smiles and gifts be passed on. Make the world a better place and you will be aligned with the spirit of incorruptible white magic at last.

10. Man feels alienated from the other kingdoms on Earth. It is time for his oneness with nature to be rebirthed. Lie on the Earth until you feel Her speak. A sentient being is She – get to know her as a friend.

11. The wind feels the hearts of the people in the street. It tells of their feelings to the forest's trees. The trees sing a song that helps people feel glad. Talk to the wind whenever you're sad. Speak too of wisdom that comes from your heart, of joyful celebration and songs of praise. This it will share with others as well.

12. Stones sing songs and if you ask they will show where to find what you seek, which way to go. Some stones will tell you, when among them you roam, to take them with you when you go home. Get to know them, for allies they are, to help with white magic you wish to wield.

13. From stars you can draw certain qualities they have. To know how they can assist, a relationship you must form. Just like the Earth, they are sentient beings. Telepathic / empathic communication knows no distance. Instantly you will hear them like a thought within your thoughts.

14. The nighttime makes magic. The moon is a friend. The sharp light from the sun interferes with intent, as do the thought-forms of others. Alone in the night, when no others are near, is the best time for magic.

15. Why do fairy folk, elfin creatures, dragons, mer people and others as well, like gemstones so much? Special powers they have, some very strong. Wear them for magic – they focus intent. Angels help gemstones and you can call on them for this. Special angels we give you that help create a response when you call on gemstones to assist in white magic.

16. Start to mix potions when the moon is full. Sing their incantations rather than just saying the words. A simple melody – just a few notes will suffice – and your potion will be stronger by far.

17. When at first you awaken the magic in you, listen as we tell you what to do. Gold is too powerful and overrides intent. Do not wear it when magic is new to you.

18. Dew has unseen properties that few can see. It rearranges old patterns that used to be. Wise ones have used it in ages gone by to erase wrinkles by letting it on the face dry.

19. Butterflies and ladybugs bring messages of gifts. They tell of presents to come into your life. Sit still for a moment, with your eyes closed tight. Then see an image of the gift to come, with your second sight.

20. Move with intent the clouds in the sky. Make a hole in them if you can. This is a good way to measure and with practice, increase the power your intent can release.

21. Laugh every day so resources can flow. Be silly and funny, as a child would play. If your window is open and your house is clean, we will come in to help you laugh – though our influence is unseen.

22. Where cell phones and microwaves and radio towers are, magic is disturbed and power is blocked in its flow. Find a quiet meadow or a moonlit cave – a place where hostile waves are far away.

23. Warm springs that rise from the earth have mud that magical properties bring. It cleanses the body of that which is old, releasing the resources the toxins did hold. More energy you'll have to do magical spells and to have clairvoyant gifts as well.

24. It is good to remember that magical powers were once held by man before life fell. They are not something you have to learn, but to remember what you already know.

Magic
of the
Fairies from Lyra

Spell 1:
Bring Forth Form

𐑥𐑩𐑯𐑛𐑩𐑮𐑪𐑒𐑦𐑯𐑩 𐑛𐑦𐑮𐑩𐑒𐑩𐑯𐑦𐑒𐑩𐑯
𐑥𐑩𐑛𐑩𐑮𐑪𐑒𐑦𐑯𐑩𐑯 𐑛𐑦𐑮𐑩𐑒𐑩𐑯𐑦𐑒𐑩𐑯𐑦

Es vaa trua, skel vu brach
Nunhur sarveesh trerurach
Bel a vees tra ve urespimarnuch
Pra u pra usbavi gerstraa plavuch

Ancient the words I speak this way
To bring to form the words I say
Shape now the image I see in my mind
Bring forth the form of one of its kind

Bersh vel es vi trua vu vi
Krenu spaau ratvi kelesh varnu
Bruach vaar ures ple hus vasarvir
Kre usnat pel uchvi verblas plasavur

That which I speak is that which shall be
By the power of the words that are given to me

Spell 2:
Return of Youth

Gelstra nu bla vish ura vechspi par ha
Glustras va urechvi utre utra vaa
Vel strach nun her brush ura plefbi parhaa
Min eres vis tra ublech travaa.

Come fill my cup with living water
That youth may return, that it be restored
Turn now this water I hold in my hand
To that which brings youth to the body of man

Bersh vel es vi trua vu vi
Krenu spaau ratvi kelesh varnu
Bruach vaar ures ple hus vasarvir
Kre usnat pel uchvi verblas plasavur

That which I speak is that which shall be
By the power of the words that are given to me

Spell 3:
Immaculate Conception

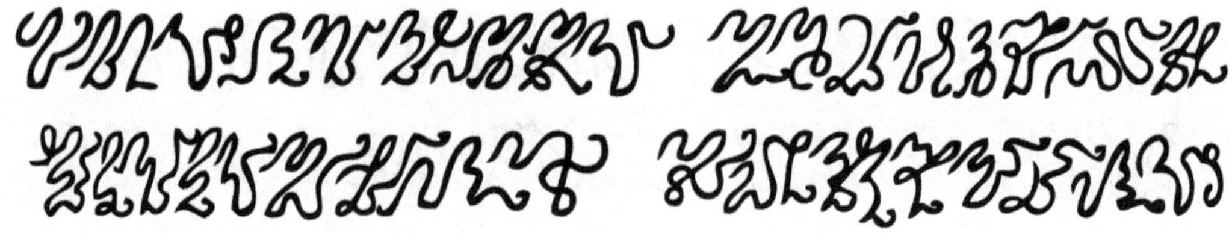

[decorative glyph script]

Varskla veesh prava manu vi sut
Kel efba uvastra minur bel va sut
Gle shtri minunechvi aruvech peravi
Vel estravaa klu bastru selvich sparari

Create your own kind by calling a child
See the little one clearly in mind
Speak these words and immaculately conceive
A babe in your womb and pregnant you'll be

Bersh vel es vi trua vu vi
Krenu spaau ratvi kelesh varnu
Bruach vaar ures ple hus vasarvir
Kre usnat pel uchvi verblas plasavur

That which I speak is that which shall be
By the power of the words that are given to me

Spell 4:
Beauty

Kre na veesh ulechbi stauret
Velskrach ba uret vavi minuset
Kle sufba elesh preusbi pravaa
Belushvi tra usvrabaa granu speluvaa

A spell of beauty for all eyes to see
But you must believe and that you shall be
Others shall see your beauty renewed
Uplifted by the sight of the beauty of you

Bersh vel es vi trua vu vi
Krenu spaau ratvi kelesh varnu
Bruach vaar ures ple hus vasarvir
Kre usnat pel uchvi verblas plasavur

That which I speak is that which shall be
By the power of the words that are given to me

Spell 5:
Grow Flowers and Plants

Ka na vush el stra blibratnavut
Vra ufba kre uch va spa rut nanuvut
Spla uvra eshvavi gel uva sperut
Nen tersh ulaefbi gerstra uvrasut

Flowers and plants will grow from these words
Bring beauty and joy as they flourish and grow
The flowers will last much longer than most
To life force and magic they are hosts

Bersh vel es vi trua vu vi
Krenu spaau ratvi kelesh varnu
Bruach vaar ures ple hus vasarvir
Kre usnat pel uchvi verblas plasavur

That which I speak is that which shall be
By the power of the words that are given to me

Spell 6:
Grow New Species of Flowers and Plants

Tre u mish ble ur ratva ulech paravi
Skel achva tru eshvi ulech pres parvi
Gre ug minur kele vishbi starur
Klech bres ur bilatrech sur het klaravur

New species will form that have never yet been
Of flowers and plants never before seen
Speak these words to the seeds in your hand
When planted new flowers will cover the land

Bersh vel es vi trua vu vi
Krenu spaau ratvi kelesh varnu
Bruach vaar ures ple hus vasarvir
Kre usnat pel uchvi verblas plasavur

That which I speak is that which shall be
By the power of the words that are given to me

Spell 7:
Abundance

𝔛𝔛𝔛𝔛𝔛𝔛𝔛 𝔛𝔛𝔛𝔛𝔛𝔛
𝔛𝔛𝔛𝔛𝔛 𝔛𝔛𝔛𝔛𝔛𝔛

Bars hut pre su na neesh va tra
Ubelechspi pra u vra sta u nit perva
Klu bechspi minureesh tra u vaa
Sta ubelvich pelushvi stel avra vaa

Great abundance is yours
Like a river it flows
Speak these words and watch it grow
First it will trickle then it will pour
Speak them again whenever it slows

Bersh vel es vi trua vu vi
Krenu spaau ratvi kelesh varnu
Bruach vaar ures ple hus vasarvir
Kre usnat pel uchvi verblas plasavur

That which I speak is that which shall be
By the power of the words that are given to me

Spell 8:
To Call in a Mate

Selbi vavechspi uret vanabi
Gleg stuch ur na menu nit
Pars klut el esh varavi
Sta uch manunaa belesh va prit
Kle stug bel uresbi, kreug beresklaa
Traug varuspi ukrech manuraa

Call in the mate that you want in your life
Write down in detail what would make the mate right
Then over the fairy writing here given
Place the list of requirements written
Speak then the words with strength from the heart
The mate is then called, never to part

Bersh vel es vi trua vu vi
Krenu spaau ratvi kelesh varnu
Bruach vaar ures ple hus vasarvir
Kre usnat pel uchvi verblas plasavur

That which I speak is that which shall be
By the power of the words that are given to me

Spell 9:
To Bring Answers

Kel vaa rutvi erch vaa uhursut
Mish tre bra as vaa urkret nan harsut
Bel ach vra uhursut kretnut hervavit
Kel esh stra uvanur brekrut nan hersut
Stra doch va uresbi nenhur varnavit

This spell awakens inspiration in you
It brings you answers, to know what to do
It brings light to a quandary, revealing the way
It helps you to know just what you should say
Still the mind when the words are spoken
That you may hear wisdom's instruction

Bersh vel es vi trua vu vi
Krenu spaau ratvi kelesh varnu
Bruach vaar ures ple hus vasarvir
Kre usnat pel uchvi verblas plasavur

That which I speak is that which shall be
By the power of the words that are given to me

Spell 10:
Freedom from Illusion

Bers anu vik pers klaa uravesbi
Gru ech vi stara ruch vi aresvi
Nin hirsh tu urachvi klauset maru net
Bil eshvi tra nech vit klaur varnaset

Free another from illusion's grip
Over a photo or name speak it
The words that are given will freedom bring
Shake loose the bonds to which he clings

Bersh vel es vi trua vu vi
Krenu spaau ratvi kelesh varnu
Bruach vaar ures ple hus vasarvir
Kre usnat pel uchvi verblas plasavur

That which I speak is that which shall be
By the power of the words that are given to me

Spell 11:
Strength in Opposition

Ulesbi kra nu va vitch ula echbi starut
Bre sut va ures nu elechvi sta arut
Bi skaa ula es na tru ul vara vaa
Kel ech vi u ach vrabi starut spaa
Menes sta uritvi keleshvi u staraa

Stand firm in the face of another's opposition
These words will give strength whenever they're spoken
The strength to know when to stand or to yield
When spoken they give you power to wield

Bersh vel es vi trua vu vi
Krenu spaau ratvi kelesh varnu
Bruach vaar ures ple hus vasarvir
Kre usnat pel uchvi verblas plasavur

That which I speak is that which shall be
By the power of the words that are given to me

Spell 12:
Harmony

Kle u vich vas urechpi staurat
Mish tra uvanesvi krechpa arurat
Skelu la u tra mish veres tra u va
Nin klu veres tra u va beles tru a mispa

To replace discord with harmony
Bring this magic to the strife
All shall dissolve instantly
That is not filled with light

Kras na sterutvi kla ushbaa heruvit
Stel uch vi u aresba helsut veruvit

But if it persists, cease to resist
For then it is meant to be
Then an insight is hidden waiting for you to see

Bersh vel es vi trua vu vi
Krenu spaau ratvi kelesh varnu
Bruach vaar ures ple hus vasarvir
Kre usnat pel uchvi verblas plasavur

That which I speak is that which shall be
By the power of the words that are given to me

Spell 13:
Restoration of Balance

Tra u ma vash ulu echbi klabusat
Vira nutvi kleush baranut trausat
Trauch bla blu va vestri elusat
Bla hutva tre u nish parvusat
Tre achbi mi lu blava ustra varbat

Restore the balance to the one in your mind
Say his name three times and you will find
That balance of emotion and mind as well
Will return to the one whom you help with this spell

Bersh vel es vi trua vu vi
Krenu spaau ratvi kelesh varnu
Bruach vaar ures ple hus vasarvir
Kre usnat pel uchvi verblas plasavur

That which I speak is that which shall be
By the power of the words that are given to me

Spell 14:
For a Beneficial Outcome

Knuch auvastra kla unet varabich
Bresh bra ma vuhet ul klet vra mastrich
Vel usvra verhat ush vra uvestra perdu
Mi es bla unesh veesh pravutaa para nos stravu

To change a path that will lead to ill
A course of action that is not of divine will
Speak these words and you can rearrange
To a beneficial outcome all will change

Bersh vel es vi trua vu vi
Krenu spaau ratvi kelesh varnu
Bruach vaar ures ple hus vasarvir
Kre usnat pel uchvi verblas plasavur

That which I speak is that which shall be
By the power of the words that are given to me

Fairy Magic for the Codes of the Heart for Manifestation

Tranuvech Pelenor u stratnava hereshvi. Ne-urishva paluna. Kre u vra hereshvi. Unut varuklem. Pre nut pre vas parvi. Stech va uvra het. Pel nus varum brish barvi. Klet vaar uset.

From far we have come, to tell you the codes. It is our gift to you. We wish to reside here. Our joining together our paths with yours will make all life flourish. Stretch your mind this day, include us in your sight.

Esh ma neesh vi ra vel, vru asbi stela hur. Kel afvra ba urutvi klesh ma nur varu bish manu resh. Estra mach mi ner va vu keles vaa. Pret sut balush vel ska u la vraa.

Give now your ear and we shall say the words to speak. They open the codes of the heart, that bring that which you desire into form. Through the magic of fairies build a new life:

*Brush aa vala vrit
Pru a nes pelu kraa
Heres vir nus parvit
Belch avru saa
Mi sulvi baresvi
Kla nur pri u saa
Belshuvanar velchvi
Rut set viles vaar
Peresh vel u satvavi
Krich barut bresh braknaa
El huf pre u selvavi
Gru staboch perus vanaa*

Kel u stri nen hurvelevi
Sta u michpre nun hersvaa
Gru va ur menunit
Heles virsh urs pravaa
Gu staa u bra efbi
Berush virsk prevaa
Garu neesh bel es efrubi
Gel stru ar nu vaach.
Paar u na presh pra vuch. Vru a buruski bel a nush. Sti arnervat kel
vis bra usut. Gra stra u sabervi esh tra ulmirat.

Impart not these words to those of impure thought. Keep them
close to your heart. For when impurities enter the fairy group - mind
through these words, fairies could die.

Granush vel es vravi heruspa ha. Krenug usva velesvi kresh tra
hur varsaa stenura velch shpi keratu. Glu staber nen hersh pra u vataa.

It takes our trust to place this gift in your hands. But if you have
been led to these words, we know your heart is true.
Use them with respect for life.

Close up of Fairy Wings.

Magic of the Earth
given by
the Fairies from Lyra

Spell 1: The Key to Start a Spell

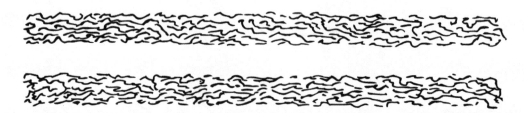

Bels brukvak blik breversbt hevelshvi akbar urklatvik nerchst helshba urutvi heresba erskruklabi. Vilnesk uret ble ufraba arha nurklitheres vilshtr ufba ursklava rech varshbi uvalefbi vanurinsk. Er klut birkspa huretpi klavavech spa-urara.

Forget not the ancient ways of yore
That which once was has been restored
By saying these words you open a door
The magic will flow for you to explore.
Say them before each spell that you do
And the magic of fairies will flow through you.

Spell 2: Satisfy Hunger

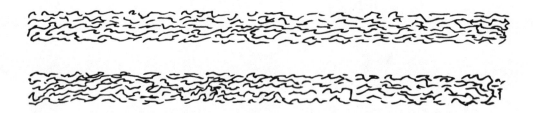

Kernakva hurik spa uvratbli asbaluk hesh tranik bliklatruk virnahikprsva ursta blshna virskva utsabaluk. Pelusvi utrabla usvanek. Krus ablut sparva nuntreshva urkirksblavi sparut shpelsvaa. Achvrasnut ulekra hirstadom branavit.

Come from the table and hunger no more
For that which you eat shall satisfy still
Feel the satiety and so it shall stay
For three meals long; what you call a day.

Spell 3: Reveal Your Charm

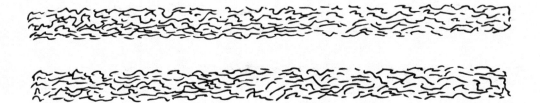

Gerchstrava barshnus helesvri vra skubaluk. Perch nit vilisk britvelsh stravuba elekstriknavirsk vla usta helsh pret prafblsk prishpra uvekspalbi klitra nus pretlufra ba helshvi varshnit elekvi avestra blatnufaferbi.

From fairies' mouths this spell does come
To bring your charm to be seen by everyone.
Let joy be felt to be by your side
The charm you have will no longer hide.

*Parek vilshvavi urabekspi valaluk
Min hur parvelshvi kranuk barnasut.*

This spell must repeat; these words you say
As you awaken upon each day.

Spell 4: Bring Friends

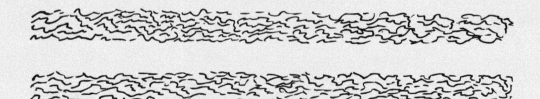

Nushbra urekbi alskva urek pri pratrnut kelsbaha nutvi.
Velskla uvra sut ba ru ek mina vra u velsh pra uversklava
hur la vik eles briknut pa u vlahu sparakletvirsh eleknu spelavra.

Speak these words to bring you friends
Those you can cherish; on whom to depend
Of like heart-energy call them to come unto you
A blessing they'll be, and you'll bless them too.

A close-up of a wood fairy with outstretched wings fills this photo.
The body is the darker blue-grey vertical part just to right of center; the head at
the top has a bark crown (instead of hair). The round globes are small fairies (elementals).

Spell 5: Avoiding Calamity

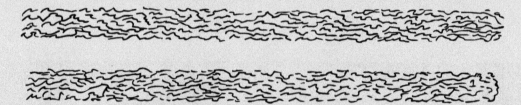

Varsvk urkslaminuvek spavaruk krasta blasut
Tre mish plauvravis pretpra hustra elekstra urhunut
Mesh tri uru ekbar uvrespa vilklarabrut prekspava
Kru niursta vilshprit heleskubris brat pravanus.

Carry this spell wherever you go
To avoid calamity that threatens to show
No longer at the mercy of the flow of another
Stay also, calamity, from the life of your brother.

Spell 6: Open the Portal to the Fairy World

Paluk brak bristrava hushpelu akvra usba helevit.
Verskra uchblereshvi krasbru ekvarastru.
Kel avri elekstraha pluprek pra ureshbi skater marnavit
sklera ubuekla vilstra u briaknabelsksut.

Come follow the trail of these words with me.
They lead to our world so you may see
Through a portal the way of the fairy world.
Practice that you may remember the sight,
For your mind may deny what is yours by right.

Spell 7: Lighten Your Load

Varechsvl hasva urablikspa urek.
Pertlahufstra marnanekspi erla urtrabilesnik sklaraa.
Perkhurk velsklavaa usetvi pirklahus pelshplik pretufla hures trahup peresnutvi veleskla.

Upon your back a heavy load;
But lighter now these words are told.
Lighter yet if you repeat it twice.
Lighter you'll be if you say them thrice.

Spell 8: Grow Seeds

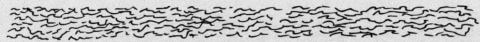

Gelva uvekstrahik manavek ekelsva retvi.
Briasva klusbra nun heresvik kra nu estra ulef palesvu sklava ruretba huruk spatlvi.
Nechtri ash vares vla ursk kla huruvas par vi baranusk pletvatlha.

Grow your seeds and they shall be
Anything you want for them to be.
The same seeds can grow many plants you will find.
See them and hold them firm in your mind.

Spell 9: Protect a Child

Birsna uretbi kilvig-nun harvasta.
Eksalbi uvlekspi kersul biles tra u varanit.
Kel achvra huresbi klashba truagnat varutreg.
Silbi nusva urva kluvabesh vi sarutrug nenvraa.

Shield your child's privacy.
Repeated once, these words prevent
The cruelty of others from piercing the shield.
Unnoticed by some is the child when in need.
Through the love of a parent form now the field.

Spell 10: Discern the Truth of Another

Haaknik peles kra u tur.
Virsknik velesh pravasur.
Graachnak elsva urs eres varvi.
Pelsh plek pra utnut spelech urs vrasvrus
pershpa pelech stra uvelesh hus nanuvrs.
Kra sut belch hirstra menenurs kelstra.

Follow another's path through his view
That you may discern his truth for you.
To understand his words to you
You must see his world through his own view.

Spell 11: Find What You Lost

Varsk varnit veles vra uvraba, erk uklat birskna hulhitsh virs kelespa.
Mir navael skla hufret ut ba urs.
Tre ukva el satru bilsh natvat berestru.
Kla u ve piles hartva ernahit.

Find what you lost. Call it to you.
By these words it shall find its way back to you.
Call while you see the image you seek.
Your voice shall call it by the words you speak.

Spell 12: Strengthen a Spell

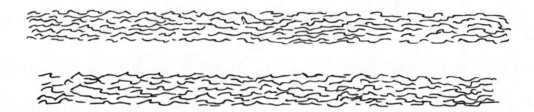

Gerch stranu valvelchspi uvra belsh abutra.
Pirs prak uvlavelchspi, usetvi kelesba ninhurs belechspa.
Nush blas bra us klenavit skel achva hers struraa.
Vrasklik belbra ushvraspurat helsut elech sutvesbi klavaa.

Speak these words over potions you make.
They only add good; they never can take.
Speak them therefore with good intent.
In your own tongue, voice what you want at the end.

To speak it in verse, the outcome you state,
Will strengthen the spell in the potions you make.
Make them from flowers and oils very pure
This works well with spells from the fairy world.

Spell 13: Loss

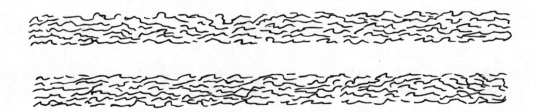

Kel es vra bi blak pra nunsu bribraket.
Pels nuchtri uvivra vi. Ska u valva dak.
Bersh nus hel sklararok spiartl hukvelsvrakra
Brik brat nut eles vivaklat uresvi harastu.
Pertl achvra varvahesh.

Find now in loss something of worth.
From something that's shed, let new now come forth.
Something is given for that which is taken.
For that which has died, let something awaken.

Spell 14: Bring Strength to Endeavors

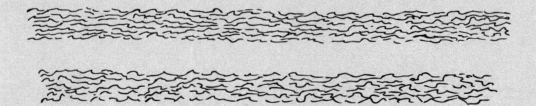

Gelstra urut hekkla ursvik blechbek selusetri hersh trabaklut nusbi erkla utvirt stelbaa. Stelalof virtl ursk manahech. Spil hersk vir kla usvra ba uch vet ersh urtlavaa.

Bring strength to endeavors by enlisting our aid
Fairy folk come where these words are said.
They know that the one who speaks them thus,
Is either a friend or one of us.

Kres nukva belish presm hurs ut travaa.
Kel virs ur ustakldos erech varavi.

A friend to all life he must surely be
To have these words only fairies may see.

Fairy Potions from Venus

Potion for Green Magic: Healing Nature

Mix and boil together:

Olive oil

Dandelion seeds

Lavender flowers

Thistle mush

Grass powder

Explanation of the Potion's Uses, Ingredients and Preparation

Green Magic is for all things natural, especially if it is broken.

If something is broken, i.e. a tree that falls after a storm, then you will want to make a big batch. If you want only to make a flower grow, you only need a small amount.

Because people are not fairies, they cannot eat this. If you will mix it and put it in a dish in your garden, we will eat it for you.

Thistle Mush is ground thistles. You will need 2 or 3, mixed with oil. You can use your olive oil because it is in your kitchen.

Grass Powder is dried grass, ground into a fine powder.

You can store this potion at room temperature for 5-10 days.

Potion for Red Magic:
Healing Cuts and Bruises

Mix and boil together:

Bendover oil

Dandelion leaves

Dragon's blood

Cherry juice

Egg whites

Explanation of the Potion's Uses,
Ingredients and Preparation

Red Magic is for if you are hurt or your friend is hurt; but it is not good to use for bones. If you have a hurt leg, i.e., a cut or torn muscle, then you will want a big batch.

You can put this on your skin for up to 5 minutes of yours, and then please wash it off. It is not a good idea to put it on your cuts so only place it near the area.

I was relieved to hear that dragon's blood refers to the dragon's blood stone (presumably ground to a powder), a "sticky" stone that resembles a dried-up blood clot.

Bendover oil is lemon juice, oregano, chili powder, jasmine oil and parsley mixed with olive oil.

You can store this potion in your ice box or in the snow for 2 days.

Potion for Blue Magic:
Cleansing or Increasing the Supply of Water

Mix and boil together:

Fish oil

Sea salt

Dandelion roots

Ocean water

Peppermint oil

Explanation of the Potion's Uses,
Ingredients and Preparation

Blue Magic is for water. If your water is dirty or you need more water, you can make this, but make a lot please because it is delicious.

Because people are not fairies, they will feel sick to eat this. If you mix it up, you can put it in your bathtub or near a puddle and we will eat it for you.

This can be stored at room temperature for 15 days.

Potion for Yellow Magic: For Remembering

Mix and boil together:

Olive oil

Dandelion flowers

Cornstarch

Egg yolk

Sugar

Explanation of the Potion's Uses, Ingredients and Preparation

Yellow Magic is for remembering what you have forgotten or lost.

You can make a lot of this and sprinkle some in your hat and in your boots so you can remember.

You can store this in your ice box for 5-10 days.

Potion for Orange Magic:
Strengthening & Healing Broken Bones

Mix and boil together:

Olive oil

Rose water

Orange peel

Mugwort

Dandelion stem

Explanation of the Potion's Uses,
Ingredients and Preparation

Orange Magic is for bones – if you have a broken one or if you need them strong. You can make a lot or a little, depending on the size of your bone.

You can place it on your skin, after you have mixed it, for up to 5 minutes and then please wash it off.

This can be stored at room temperature for 15 days.

Potion for Pink Magic:
For Love

Mix and boil together:

Olive oil

Peach juice

Sugar

Rose petals

Rose water

Dandelion flower

Dandelion root

Explanation of the Potion's Uses,
Ingredients and Preparation

This is in case you have a lover, you love your friends, or you love yourself; because it is not a good idea to not express love. Please make a lot of this one because it is a very delicious dessert.

When you are mixing this, please remember to think of the ones you are loving and then please put it in a very beautiful bowl. You can set it out anywhere you like for 20 days; but please be aware that it probably won't last for 20 days, because we will eat it by then.

Potion for Purple Magic:
Ease Stress and Tiredness

Mix only:

Olive oil
Bendover oil
Apple peel
Dandelion juice
Aloe vera

Explanation of the Potion's Uses,
Ingredients and Preparation

Purple Magic is for when you have stress, or you are tired and you need to rest. It is good to mix this beside the Dream Magic potion if you are planning on going to bed.

After you have mixed it, place in a bowl and put beside your chair or beside your bed.

This should not be kept for longer than a day.

Potion for Quick Magic:
To Speed up Things

Mix only:

Olive oil

Lavender oil

House dust

Peanut butter

Honey

Explanation of the Potion's Uses,
Ingredients and Preparation

Quick Magic is for when you need something done 'speedy quick'. Mix these ingredients up very fast with your hand or a spoon. While you are mixing, think of what you want done. Place it on a bowl or a dish and we will eat it right away.

This should not be kept for longer than a day.

Potion for Plug Magic: For When You are Stuck

Mix only:

Olive oil

Molasses

Honey

Chewing gum

Yellow Magic potion

Quick Magic potion

Explanation of the Potion's Uses, Ingredients and Preparation

Plug Magic is for if you are stuck. Mix and then bury it in your yard right away please. Do not store this at all. Thank you.

Potion for Success Magic

Mix together and boil:

Yellow Magic potion

Green Magic potion

Pink Magic potion

Coconut milk

Explanation of the Potion's Uses, Ingredients and Preparation

Success Magic is for if you are ready for success of your person or something else.

After you mix this one, please put it in a dish and place it in your kitchen near your cooking space for up to 10 days.

Potion for Dream Magic

Mix only:

Olive oil

Coconut milk

Blueberry juice

Lavender oil

Explanation of the Potion's Uses, Ingredients and Preparation

Dream Magic is for when you like a type of dream. You will need to remember what to say when you are finished mixing. (I asked whether she meant that at the end of mixing the potion, one needed to announce what type of dream it will bring. She answered, "Yes, please, please, Miss!")

This works very well alone and also with Purple Magic. After you have mixed this and you have said what kind of dream you like, place in a bowl beside your bed.

Do not keep this for longer than a day.

Potion for 3 H Magic:
Make things 3 times hotter

Mix only:

Olive oil
Chili powder
Poppy seeds
Paper ashes

Explanation of the Potion's Uses,
Ingredients and Preparation

3H Magic is for when you would like to make something three times hotter. When you are mixing, please remember to think of what you want hotter. Then place the potion in a dish and we will eat it. If you wouldn't mind, please leave a glass of water beside the dish because it will be hot on our tongues.

Do not keep this longer than a day.

Potion for Cold Magic

Mix only:

Water
Banana peel
Pine needles
Oak bark

Explanation of the Potion's Uses, Ingredients and Preparation

Cold Magic is for if you would like to freeze something in your life – only if you like it.

You do not need to mix a lot of this; but when you are done mixing, put it in a dish in your freezer or you can put it in the snow for 30 days. (I asked whether one should put a written piece of paper in the mixture before freezing, stating what one wanted to freeze. The answer: "Think of it as you stir the mixture with your spoon.")

Potion for Yellow Eyes Magic:
To See Beautiful Sights

Mix together and boil:

Olive oil

Peppermint oil

White cat fur

Flour

Explanation of the Potion's Uses, Ingredients and Preparation

Yellow Eyes Magic is for when you would like to see very beautiful sights. This is an easy one, but please use scissors to cut your cat's fur because if you yank on it he will get mad, then you will be in trouble. Also, please ask him if it's OK so you are not rude.

This should be placed in a bowl on the floor, but watch out so your cat doesn't eat it.

You can keep it there for 10 days.

Potion for Red Hand Magic:
To Discern the Truth

Mix together and boil:

Olive oil

Oregano oil

Chili powder

Raspberry juice

Bendover oil

Explanation of the Potion's Uses,
Ingredients and Preparation

Red Hand Magic is for if your friend is being sneaky and you would like to know the truth.

When you have finished mixing this, put some in your friend's garden. You can store this for 10 days inside your icebox.

Magic
of the
Fairies from
Andromeda

Prehina — Candles of Wisdom

Candle 1 Secret 1:
The Secrets of Music

Vils klanach ve rush, u trua virhat
Spelech vi blush, uretvi visach
Belesh bliva urvahet bivarit
Elesh mi saverhet nun spaverhit

No clocks there are, nor time , nor space
But frequency changes mark the pace
Every hour it changes. Twelve times this is so
It then repeats; and like before it goes

Mech priha verushvi skalet uvervaa
Belech vi asvarv herut velespaa
Krenuch mi staber herut elestu
Belsh ikvanaver herut milveshtu

For music you play or the songs that you sing
To enhance your life and joy to bring
Trace the songs of birds all day long
How each hour they change the tones of their song

Besh aber var hech sutra va ura
Belesh pra-ut savar velsh averstra
Kels mich pauret velskatel urit
Kruag mi nanastru urech valabit

Then emulate them and the change that occurs
The right music at the right time emotions will stir
Sound is a clock, frequency is time
Learn this secret and power is thine

Candle 1 Secret 2:
Balance through Color

Versh echva urusvi keles vrivar
Spel uvra huch spavi ulech spar
Nun spesbi klesh avri uvravar

Color is tone made visible to see
If you play in the forest too much of the green
The soul will feel that excess has been

Branuch veles nustrava heres tra u vat
Shpi uvra uvresbi herut sar vu tat
Belanoch verklut uravespi strahur
Keles vi nuch vravi tre usbanaklur

In the forest play the tones that are red
By yellow or blue, too, the soul will be fed
In deserts of course the green will be fine
Each climatic region has its own music sublime

Candle 1 Secret 3:
Restoration of the Tones of Emotion

Kruavestri paruch minuvestri baha
Pluanuchvi uvavrastu, pelesh vraha
Sutl achvranastuk elechbi stra-uhet
Peleshvi manabrut upelsbi straunet

Where tones are missing, illusion abides
Sound distorted, illusion of illness resides
Through music these tones can be fully restored
The missing tones once more can be yours

Vera biskirat utra selvi shpat
Pelech vi bru utra vis abruspat
Helech inor sabu helspi varanech
Eres vi isbavar struvet manure

But now as you know, each time of day
A tone reigns supreme, so find when to play
The tone that you need, the flaw to heal
The sounds will restore and better you'll feel

Candle 1 Secret 4:
The Secret of Music to Balance the Emotions

Versh vrasna uber fat heles par vi
Klech esh bra uversat hels bravari
Plech plaa uhurs tre a varavi
Skeluch paruf us va ba tra u vi

Twelve notes there are in the scale that you know
Each note promotes an emotion's flow
Twelve pairs there are of emotions true
The key of the music will choose one for you

Verskrachva urish manuhetvi sklauraa
Versatva uvish treuach manuraa
Pulunuchvi plaret uresvi pelaa
Varu helvink uskach ururaa

Emotions must pulse, the two in each pair
In the same way the music must pulse here and there
Proactive at times, then receptive again
The male and the female this represents

Belech struavi vaa heshpi kleraa
Strua varvit ulech bi klarit

When frequencies pulse, awareness will raise
Your life will become a song of praise

Candle 2 Secret 1:
Balance Through Play — The Secrets of Play

Varshvi sklurechba ulesbi varhaa
Pret priu nanavish uklechva baraa
Pelesnu haresvaa uruklechbi strauvaa
Vruspret unesbi ulech klauraa

Play is active, it is often thought
But the other half of play must be sought
As in all things, balance must be
For play to deliver its gifts to thee

Gelech shtra u vespi blauch strauhaa
Tru bela vechspi uret beleshtraa
Minur sarvu geleshva uret palanich
Streu bra velespaa klet branavich

Play must be active and passive as well
Comprehend this and then its secrets I'll tell
For play the blockages of mind will release
Emotions, too, it will set free

Candle 2 Secret 2:
Achieving Excellence

Kranish his pelech vu
Arnu belsh blich manastru
Kel vi vaa u vilistraa hik
Belu peleshtru na ur blavik

Is it that you wish to excel?
Then I exhort you to listen well
Play will help your accomplishments grow
For one promotes the other you know

Kelus vistra velus es
Ninhur barkla varlu plesh
Brisk bra krut u nanuvirt
Elch u vastraa mil planirt

The harder you play, the more you achieve
Where the other is not, the one cannot be

Candle 2 Secret 3:
Assistance in Growing Plants

Estra heshu velech nut
Asvru belstru stranik blut
Pelesh vi ustrachbi haa
Klut ma sutvaa verestraa

The wee folk want assistance from you
If you will help, here's what to do
Plants will grow wherever you play
But be consistent and play each day

Peshvis belechvi hares tra uni
Birs bra uvravespi ulech pranabi
Kelsut manurim ura vespi trahaa
Elech vra nutvi klash uvrabaa

Nature withers when ambition is blind
When work and strife is all we can find
The desire to revel must go hand in hand
Inner balance inevitably leads to restoring balance throughout the land

Candle 2 Secret 4:
Helping Children Read Well — The Secret of Play

Bra brush branu vespi ulech minaru
Belesh vivaspra, uret klanavu
Kreshbi uvra spuch u vra vespi aruk
Nun spelvi achvra sut hel sut velvravuk

To understand concepts, relationships see
To see them, you first must cognizant be
Of maps of space, of which there are two
One is within, and one outside you

Kirshaber verut urna vechspi verhat
Klush aber hurvavet urs varuspach
Nun stelbi u lachvra urhespi verluch
Spi ura vilstravaa uklech varna bruch

These maps are formed at the age of five
No sooner nor later, however hard you strive
These maps are formed in children through play
Through running and jumping and playing each day

Velskla ubrahupspi urech tra-uni
Velupshpa kreruspravi speluch varuni

Without these maps their letters aren't right
Play therefore helps them to read and to write

Candle 3 Secret 1:
The Secrets of Work — Balance

Barsklu hirs vir klaravi urech sparaklu
Brish ubra hestruvi minach varaklu
Bel astra-uvach spirabich klauret
Min hurs u strauvat kleru baru-set

First it builds up, then it tears down
For it is based on a concept profound
That all that goes out, must also come in
Everything pulses without and within

Kelefba hurukvi spela hur varsit
Kels us vra achvrabi ules balastrit
Mish pres usvraresbi klunisvra varha
Vel pris pra evreshbi klech uvrastat

After twelve hours of work that you've done
A time of destructuring must be begun
If not, the work you have done falls apart
Then decay in the cells of your body will start

Fru vit uvra lechspi minur klabusat
Velech pra-uvrabi hel ush varstat

Be therefore wise and work not too hard
And thus it shall be that you will go far

Candle 3 Secret 2:
The Secrets of Work — Fueled by Joy

Kerslu ech vra sut nit het valasbi
Erch klu achvra kru varasbi
Klesh nit alsva ech vrabit
Klusva hechbi stalach nit

When work isn't fueled by the joy of your heart
It can't to the cosmos benefit impart
It needs emotion pure and true
To ripple through all and return to you

Gir stra urechbi hirut paruve
Mish klia struavet belech klaruve

A loveless task brings lack your way
A spiral that's inward must bring decay

Varstra minuhet ula vech bileshtra
Vilichpe uruf paresh mishtra vilesta
Kruag ur nuf parvu klulech brich brasta
Mirnug ules varasbi sparuch veleshtra

Filled with love for the work you do
The benefits spiral away from you
Causing increase wherever it goes
Like a life-giving river, its blessings will grow

Candle 3 Secret 3:
Success

Krech staber uretvi herush barnustach
Viles ba krugelva nur bish plavach
Sterut steura urnavesh pla-ura
Veluchva urishpravi kleru vanusta

What doesn't go forth through the cosmos to bless
Does not produce results that are best
For increase can't come to work that is done
To the self-centered benefit of only one

Candle 3 Secret 4:
Energy through Food & Clothes

Virsh na drua velsklat uvefri barklut
Hilch treva helsat ubravechspri barut
Milklish vil es rutvaba sklura harnestu
Ules viachvraba erus stanavuch

The clothes that you wear, the food you eat
Must be made with love or they're incomplete
When there's a hole in the web of life
Something withheld, one must pay the price

Kraug minerva klaug starech
Elsh planu vanabi brish brach varech

Energy therefore is taken away
From the user of products made in this way

Candle 4 Secret 1:
Making Spells Successful

Virskra uvravechspi urlut veleskra
Mish tre uvra heresvi erlut mishpata
Klesut vilva velesbi klarut minarech
Starok uvra velespi klasut virnastech

How long, do you say, will it take to appear
As I do the magic you've given me here
Three things it takes to successfully do
The magical spells we have given to you

Preshaber verut usterva barut
Pelesh vi nutvi uklet banasut
Perch nis vis uklat vraber usutvi vrabu
Elesh vi nut vrabit urech ustrabu

The three ingredients to successful spells
Love, joy and energy work very well
Neutral, negative and positive aspects are they
Important are they in the part they play

Barach vi nut uluhelshbi sklaru
Kel ufvra vishpavi urech manaru
Sul mish pliklat uretvi miret
Pres uver ushvraba ures manavet

Each has a role in the magic you do
From the fairies comes this message to you
Blame not the spell if it should elude you
For you need these three keys the spells to do

Candle 4 Secret 2:
The Secrets of Magic

Pelesh vi staber elechvra urahet
Vistra us aver nuret manarut
Pelesh vru verestra uchvi vra starom
Kru mich palesh vavi unich vil stalom

Love will hasten the effects that you want
Thus love what you do, that which will come
Love these secrets that have come from so far
Love one another and whomever you are

Candle 4 Secret 3:
Promoting Magic

Granuch veresh hers parvaa
Kru nutvi steruk belch us vas branutaa
Kelsh shtra uvra uter brish brak hernavu
Klusat uvra bers krauta heruk kresnavu

In doing magic, building blocks you'll need
Joy attracts them; pulls them in with speed
The raw material from which to produce
Is the cosmic life force for you to use

Bilch vra nutvi staus vilsh achvra staruk
Erus bra skruvrabi helsut manavuk

Joy is negative and thus can receive
The elements to build what you conceive

Candle 4 Secret 4:
Drawing Energy into a Spell

Gluchfrak banasut mileshpa trahut kelesvaa
Prufbak urespavi belich venestraa
Berechpaa uhustravi klesh us va us baktaa
Mir pla urespavi klusut menestaa

Energy comes in three forms[5] as you know
One is a ray of light, the other the force that moves
The one we mean is an element, one of creation's needs
Permeates everything, everywhere, residing all around thee

Kulushbri u brech va brut
Stelech a u-vra banasut
Peleshviplaa ureshbi varuch
Stelech pri vaa uvanabruch

Like a sponge, and through your skin
Energy without, draw within
Absorb as much as you can stand
Then raise it up to the pineal gland

Ku ulu steavit blish blech parvaa
Krechnut stu avravit uhursh u starvaa
Nin skel banasut uvra vespi varspet
Skle hur uvra vanashet klu ut hurspavet

Raise it up like with a drinking straw
Suck in your breath, as up you draw
The energy into the center of your head
Hold it there as your spell is said

5. See "What is Energy" in *The Ring of Truth*.

Bra bis klanuvar uru asba sta-arut
Krechna uvravar uruesbi banaklut
Elech prenusva uklesh vanabik
Stelsut uvra vaspava uret manablik
Greknach velhispi urech vanabel
Eras vernukvi sparuch eskradel

But how to release that which you hold
Listen well as the secret is told
Like a sponge that you squeeze, muscles contract
Deep in the head with your eyes tilted back
Pour it into the spell you have said
Releasing energy from inside your head

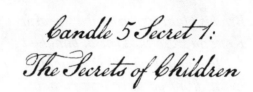

Candle 5 Secret 1:
The Secrets of Children

Gruchsta bileshbi stanarok verskraurit
Bil bech vra uvresbi bla-uch stanarik
Grubilshpa urechbi veluskra virskravi
Belshpa va uvravik urech spanavi

That which once was, now has been changed
It only is fair that gifts are exchanged
Formerly children took perception at birth
Took away from their parents that which was theirs

Krustra bilech spara elechsva uhurutvi klanaruk
Trehur pa ulesva uhur vanastik
Pelva uhusvri urechspi elesva
Ru-setvi u keleshva u ret banastik

With each child, a little light lost
Thus the children came at a cost
But now this is changed, light is now gained
And so for each child the parent is paid

Candle 5 Secret 2:
Freedom from Belief Systems

Bruestrava klu-uhespri brech treuna varablit
Kluesh upriviva urech strauvit
Kelesh vi nutvi varuech ustravaa
Glu-uvra hechspavi uset varivaa

Written in the Book of Life; the following has been said
Parents no longer lock children into belief systems that are dead
No longer are assemblage[6] points fixed after birth
Setting free the children of planets like Earth

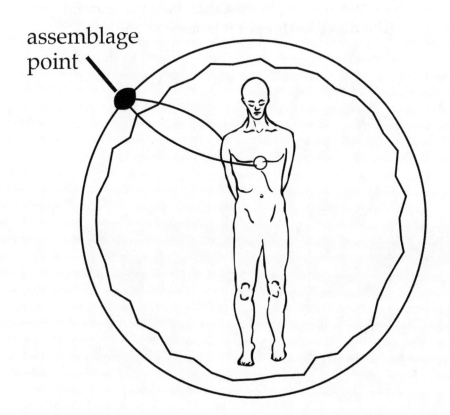

assemblage
point

6. The assemblage point is a ball of light on the edge of the fields around the bodies, or fields of man. See *Secrets of the Hidden Realms*.

Candle 5 Secret 3:
Freedom to See into Other Realms

Kelshtru vitva kla avuhet
Mishtra hutvi erch vanabet
Klesvaa struanach brusba avruvaa
Berchva husbi kles u avruhaa

Because the assemblage point is not locked anymore
The children can see far more than before
Into realms unknown they will freely gaze
With sights to delight and bring joy their way

Barechpi unesh varuvis uspalvi
Krech aver sutravat shpaluch ushstabi

No longer does aught exist that could make afraid
And thus now this gift is brought to our babes

Candle 5 Secret 4:
The Gift the Child Brings

Gel aver veruchspi klanuber versat
Pelachva uhesvrafat staruch varabi
Plesh rut uravespi erech tranavu
Ubla va spechvabi ures trana du

Four minutes after birth, once prison bars made
Before, those that touched programmed the babes
Giving beliefs, even though seldom right
That colored the vision of the child's whole life

Glanuch starechvi urstru urarat
Pelsh bich vel uvrava uhur avrustak
Pel nuchvi veles vra vaa speluch vilanut
Hersh pri u ech vrabi uher aversut

But now the child, during this crucial time
Bestows upon others vision sublime
Those that touch will now receive
Innocent vision and faith to believe

Candle 6 Secret 1:
Family Groups

Vra ma vit hesh traug vi nach
Pelsh ubrav uret vis ba vach
Truag manur uluvesbi trahaa
Kelesh vi tra ma nug vis u bataa

Previously chosen based on that which opposed
Families often did not feel like home
Opposite energies much friction brought
Through discomforts were the lessons taught

Skel achva ureshpi kelustru mispataa
Vis usbavespi ukluch veleshtraa
Baruk nin hur set vravi ulechbi strauhaa
Stel uvra veshpavi uklech vish bavaa

But growth now comes through support
Through loving examples learning is brought
Families now are chosen this way
When energy is the same, together they'll stay

Candle 6 Secret 2:
Balance and Strength

Bri-esh tra u-va ulavechspi travu
Klesh bra-u vespavi kluach manatu
Bel hik us bavaa minestra stravaa
Kelush bri uch vrabi stel us vasbaa

Decreed it has been by Mother's own voice
That those drawn close, come by energy's choice[7]
But because all are turning to light, understand well
While like ones are attracted, some distance is held

Glistrekvi kranech uhus pelesnur
Klanu vi bres tra u vavrablur
Stel huf ufbra uchvi stelelut beleshtur
Kla u vra vespavi veluch manestur

This will erase co-dependency's bane
We will love, but without neediness and pain
Inter-dependency offers support that we need
Balance and strength our sustenance will be

7. Recent cosmic changes have same energies attracting, but same light repelling. To keep lightbeings from repelling one another, Mother decreed that heart energy should always slightly exceed each person's light quotient.

Candle 6 Secret 3:
The Growth of the Child

Velshpri urech parave ulavek
Steru urat vravi kle-ug nanivuk
Blesh bli uvra vechspi ura heruvit
Kelesh vi uchvrava ures vanabit

At birth of a child both parents rejoice
Both want to be with the baby by choice
Instinct is strong to support mother and child
The father delights to be by their side

Stravink helsvra sutbravi elles tra uravech
Hersut bel uchstrabi uret manavech
Lu stravik elsh nut trava uklet viles ves
Uch miu strek vravi uret vana bes

Thus for a time in the life of a babe
New life supported and dependency reigns
As the baby grows bigger, tries things on his own
Father and mother teach by example shown

Pleug ustra milleshpa nurhut vilstravaa
Kleug vla ustravi herut varestraa
Ma pri-eg ulvesbi kliu vanastat
Bilch ples u verarut u nes viushtat

Co-dependence though to independence turns
As the older child now on his own must learn
And as he sets forth to make his own home
Inter-dependence shows he is not all alone

Veraski vivach utrechbi speraa
Belesh vi blich us tru vereraa
Pluach varavich uvra struvra verhaa
Varnech vrablik ures pre va haa

Candle 6 Secret 4:
Blessing to Support Mothers-to-be

We ask now a question to see if you know
What happens when to pregnant mothers you show
Support and assistance in her time of need
If you don't know, then please give heed

Klunech stri stravek ureshbi klauraa
Strechva vra blik usut varuhaa
Ninubirsh staurechbi kleuvas stauraa
Minuvech stau vesbi u klet stararaa

That which you shelter and offer to help
Is actually a gift you give to yourself
The blessing you get, rejuvenation by name,
In the measure you give, that you will gain

Pilistur klava vra u vech parlaa
Spispa varet uresh klu a vaa

And now end the candles of wisdom we give
May they bring wisdom to the way that you live

The Shield to Safeguard the Magic of the Fairies

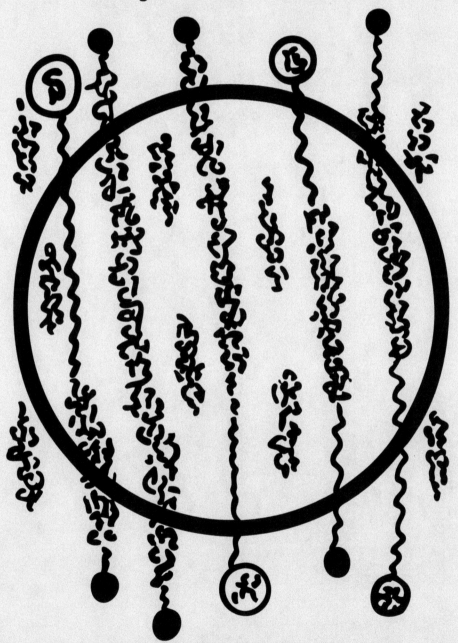

Mishtavich siblevi eres truhanes suvatvi

Magic of the Horse Tribes

Spells from the Horse Libraries

Spell 1: Abundant Prosperity

Baarnavik hereshvaa straunit bil
Harnaves klaunak birplakvi stauvil
Stua vra vet urnahespi plaktaa
Elekna hustrava, setvi arustaa

Nin haravik hespi elklasvravaa ustavi
Pelek nun hustavi, belesh us tra–uni

Every night say these words and trace the sigil too
Trace the sigil and say the words you must do
Then in the dream time let the magic work for you
Repeat this incantation and let prosperity accrue

Sigil for Abundance

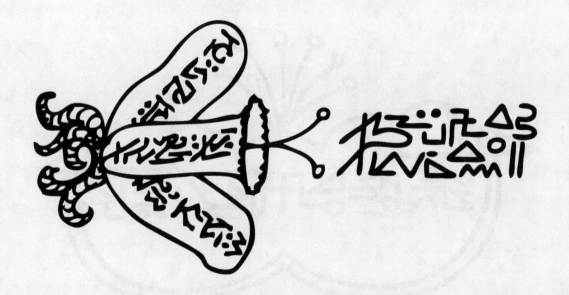

Spell 2: Stability

Eres berenish strau bla–uvravit spar hu
Klaunar vasvrahit ustuavech staranu
Bileshpla uhuru nunavit, stelevech uhaspi klanaa
Birsh branavit urespa kla–unach, ustetvi keleshbi uspaa

From my navel to the life force center let there be
A tube that between these centers reaches
Let the navel's chakra with life force supplied
Stability to my body provide

Through the tube let life force flow
From the navel to the whole body it will go

Sigil for Stability

Spell 3: Increased Personal Power

Krabavik hersatu nanech sersavat
Ekspa mishtek herelech krasvanit
Sikva bilshprech sebarechvi

Let my solar plexus draw from Source's supply
The power I need to accomplish what is mine
To powerfully affect all life for good
To wield the power that I should

Power come my being to fill
Let my destiny with power be fulfilled

Sigil for Increased Personal Power

Spell 4: The Sword of Discernment

Aklach ubaveshvi. Heresta usbavi
Nin uba eresklat, nus prehes vravi
Kelesh ustaakvi, beres hurnastaa
Elesh uvrichbavi, ukleshvi ustavaa

Piruvak nech ba sur, hereshvi usklavaa
Vilesh uhech stravaa, bilesh hustabraa

Sword of Discernment in the sacred halls
Come from the libraries, come as I call
Cut through the mist that around me lies
Show me the heart of truth that there does lie

Sigil for Sword of Discernment

Spell 5: Release

Hernak herevi survat hus
Nenhurch pa uklesvi steravi vavuch
Bilestaa belspravaa elekvi struvaa
Keleshvi erestaa nun herpirsh pravaa uverestaa praavi
Kilbasplaahur setvi aranit

Release that which has energy cost
Restore energy that has already been lost
Let me not hold to that which does not serve
Free from fetters that bind, let me live
Cut now the cords, release the ties
Let energy and self-empowerment be mine

Sigil for Release

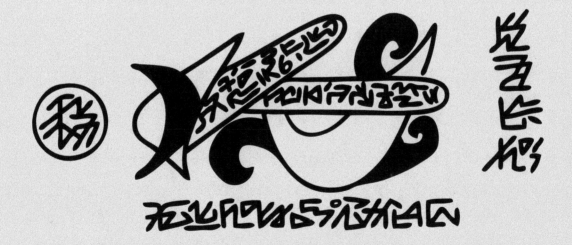

Spell 6: Access the Source of All Magic

Pelspraa pruvahit nechpaa aluvish
Kelesut uherespi ukleshva haruvit
Nin birispaa uklesvravi kelsvaa arunat
Selechvaa uhereshpa ukleshvaa aruvit
Viriknaa uhastravaa sutvi balaluch
Ninhurstaa ubelavich nin hurbavach uselvusta

A sigil there is to place on your left
On the right another sigil to be set

Profound the power that moves this way
A part of this power this spell can relay
Tap into this pulse as Mother's heart beats
As the sigils are placed and you sit in between

Back and forth - each library a source
The power pulses through you on its course
To do this each day will your power increase
That you may be empowered and all impotency cease

Sigils for the Source of all Magic

The Libraries of the Rose

Place on your left

The Libraries of the Divine Masculine

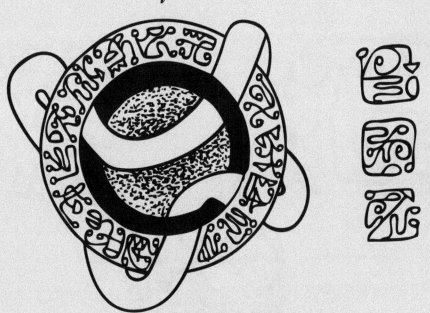

Place on your right

*When the Divine Masculine and the Divine Feminine
are one, white magic in the physical form is born.*

Spell 7: Enhance the Magic of a Wand

Minspaa ukra selvuvat. Herechstaa ubravavit
Kelherestaa usbaa min perpataa. Ulustavach heruhit
Menesh prêt praa hers klaavu bach
Bilis trenahur ulvaa bresut plakta
Vilesh nuchpi kelestaa. Treunaa vra vista huch
Bliblesh prêt praa min persatvi kel astruch

Three sigils I give you for magic to gain strength
For a magic wand, along its length
Write them in ink over which these words are said
But write them each in one color; one blue, one yellow, one red
These sigils are given, for requested they'll be
By a glorious embodied Fairy queen

Call the power of the sigils when their names you repeat

Kerachni

Vileshpa

Haruhek-vi

108

Spell 8: Pull in Assistance

Kiritrach velvash praktaa. Estavir mi-eshta bis
Kelnit uvra vri. Bla-uhesprataa uklat vranit
Selvi eckstaa helevish travaa
Piritruch veleshbi ste-uklesvi hursvrataa

All that is without lies in the fields within
This you must know before you begin
Each kingdom of beings, one and all
Has a sigil you use upon them to call
Given by the Mother for the world of man
To aid in life's tasks, to call with the sigils you can

Sigils of the Kingdoms

Given by the Mother to Call Upon for Their Assistance

Focus on the sigil while saying the incantation.
Close by signing it in the air or tracing it on the page.

 The Fairy Kingdom — For use in smaller magical tasks

 The Angelic Kingdom — Call on them for all tasks except cerebral ones like bookkeeping

 The Elfin Kingdom — For help in deterring hostile actions in others

 The Twitches — For large tasks (like dragons)

 The Mer People — Powerful magic for larger tasks

The Darklings — For use in getting past information

Sigils of the Kingdoms

The Giants — Powerful magic in all larger tasks

The Pegasus — They have much power to build something new

The Unicorns — For healing and comfort

The Lords of Light — For large, deductive, cerebral tasks

The Nitzkabelavek — To create invisibility shields

The God Kingdom — To help the Earth and nations

The Spirit Realms — For support of self and family

Spell 9: Creating an Alliance with Nature

Vrivravat bit hespi, krach statvi ursvra kluhavet
Kelshpa ustra bra vit praunatvravet
Kirech nutvi stel vra bi virestat
Nitva bli-esh prahur. Nin burchra usba stetvi verstat
Pi-ilekvravi stra helesvi brechbra klas vra bi
Rutsa ba ulech heresh vilesba vi

With these words a connection make
With nature – then everywhere you its presence take
As you carry its peace inside
In you its purity constantly abides

But be aware as you carry nature's presence in you
That while it beneficially affects you, you impact nature too

Sigil to Create an Alliance with Nature

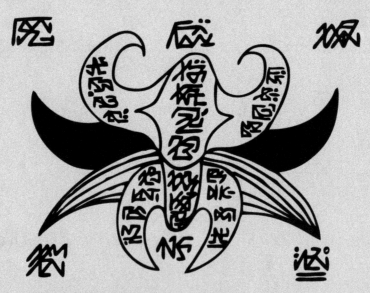

Belek spavi urechvi hurahaspavi

Within lies the secret of nature

Spell 10: Augmenting Another Spell

Kars varisvra, bilesh ustra kraunach
Stela ruspa kra satvi arurech spra vach
Nus kelesbi ustet heres usta vravit
Helsh prakpraa nus harasvi ernasit
Usma nanet. Viritvaa klavusa
Bri es traa u na kel esh hustra vaa kelesna

Let this spell, a gift from the Mother
Be used to augment the purpose of another
Add these words and the sigil too
To the words of another spell given to you
Then good you do by proxy, for one
Will then affect not just him but everyone

Sigil to Augment Another Spell

Nechpararet uhasvi usbaa klanenuvish

What benefits one will do so for all

Spell 11: Dissolving Appearances of Illusion

Krachvi nunespra ha viris nustra bli ech avruset
Ubilesna sparuspa ha. Kla estrauselvi sta achvruset
Pirtre blu as vravaq. Nin triu as klavrubat
Ekletnusba herstra es uvrabit nun helesh pruvasat

To that which is unreal, command that it be gone
See it disappear like mist before the sun
With these words it must reveal its face
Banish all that is unreal from lingering in your space
But the power of these words can do much more than this
They can dissolve the unreal; it no longer exists

Sigil for Dissolving Appeareances of Illusion

Aranush helechsvrivas kluhaneshvavi

Unreal, reveal thyself

The Shield to Safeguard the Magic of the Horse Tribes

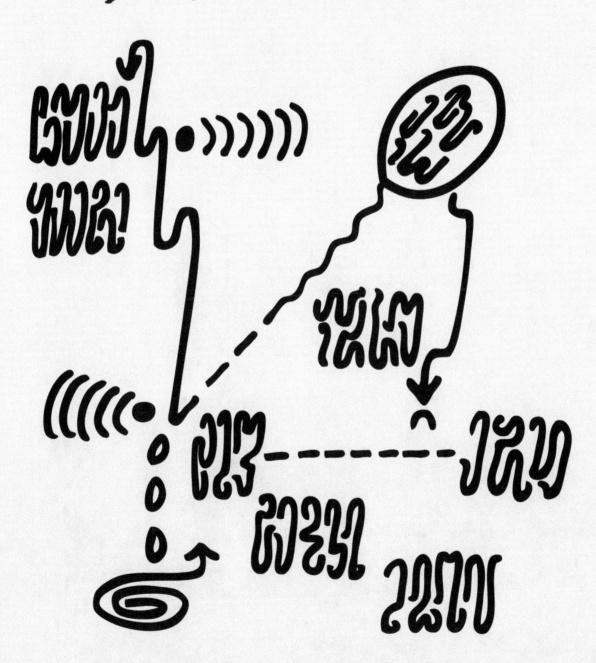

Akra misunech versenut heret perevisvanu

Magic
of the
Mer People

Introduction to the Mer Clans

To fulfill the purpose of the Mother Goddess, namely to restore white magic to the human kingdom, more kingdoms than just the horse races and fairy realms participated. Kingdoms such as the Mer clans and other forgotten kingdoms have brought forth, willingly and gladly, not only the sacred objects they have guarded, but the secrets they have held.

The statement 'knowledge is power' has far more truth to it than generally realized. Perception gained, yields personal power and that in turn elevates consciousness. The gift of knowledge shared by these magical kingdoms is therefore, a gift of consciousness to mankind.

The magic shared, tests our willingness to receive and appreciate what is given, to take seriously the sacred responsibility that goes hand in hand with the magic. Only then will we be able to receive the rest of the knowledge held in the magical kingdoms.

The Remaining Mer People

Few there are that remain of the once proud race of the Mer clans, each traveling within separate areas of the oceans. Only fifty of the Oonim Clan are left. They are the ones that can breathe both under water and in the air. In the last days of November 2006, they received their magic from Mother.

The Vraanim Clan are the only ones that have had magic throughout the ages. Of the Vraanim, only twenty-five are left. The Waaroom, like the Oonim, have just received their magic from Mother. The Waaroom are smaller than the other clans; there are only twenty-five of them left.

Descriptions of Mer People

The people of Mer look a lot like humans, with big, wide human-like eyes of dark blue. They have broad facial features, a small nose and forehead, and ears close to their heads. They grow hair and, like humans, the men have facial hair. They all have webbing between their fingers. Some wear clothes while others do not. The three clans do have specific distinguishing features, however, as outlined below.

The Oonim

The Oonim are six feet tall. This is the only clan who breathe both below and above the water, and so they have only one fish-like gill on each side of the neck. The skin and hair of the Oonim are various shades of green. They have a fish-like tail that starts at the area of the knees with wide and short tail fins.

The Waaroom

The people of the Waaroom Clan are only three feet tall, with smooth, peach-colored skin. As they breathe only underwater, they have two gills on each side of their neck. Their hair is black. Their feet are about twice as long as a human's, with five elongated toes that are webbed, much like frog's feet. They have no nails on their fingers or toes.

The Vraanim

The people of this clan are quite similar to the Oonim, also measuring six feet in height. Their tail differs in that it starts at the hip and has one bendable joint where our knees would be. Their tail fins are narrower and longer than those of the Oonim. Like the Waaroom, they have two gills on each side of their neck. The Vraamin have white hair.

Depiction of Oonim
and Waaroom Clan Members

Oonim Clan Member

They have one fish-like gill on each side of the neck. Their fish-like tail starts at the area of the knees, with wide and short tail fins.

Waaroom Clan Member

They have two gills on each side of their neck. Their feet are about twice as long as a human's with five elongated toes.

A Key to be Able to Contact the Mer People

Place in front of you when calling them. The top inscription reads:

Once more let the door between man and Mer be opened.

Given by the Waaroom. The top inscription is a very ancient form of a Lemurian dialect.

Spell for Sacred Object 1: The Crystal (or Glass) Ball

Oosh vaoom mee eesh vaaoovavee paaoovaamaanii ooee huuhem. Waa vii staoo bieesh naanuu mii staa vii hiiee baa oo heem. Viieemii oo aavi shaaoohem paa klii stavaaeesh piiooheem baa vaa.

Let me sleep in the arms of the sun
Lay me down till three days are done
On a rock on the ocean floor where the water is shallow
And the sunlight pours through
There will I rest till I leave with you

Shushaamee ubeesh viaa staa waa spullheem sha uaashva sklaa uresh bee vaa uu naa sishvii plaauuhem. Staa huu mii aevaa sasoom wii lii plee aahuuna vaveesh hieesh staa voom.

For half a day, send your images of mind into the heart of my crystal depths. Then speak these words that I might become a conduit of knowledge from the central sun.

"Pirsnaa vii vaa ures klaa. Nanuhesh baooliibaa aa. Siilee soo eesh vaa bii eesh naa u biish. Virtluu beebaavaa oo neem bii staroom"

Vaaloosh beesh viirs staa vii pervaa nice staa baa vee oo aa stii baa naa vee keloosh hirsh vii staa baa laa miee saa buu haa uueesh ullvim pisvareem bi aa vaa staa rim

Now carry me with you like a babe in your arms
Sleep cradled around me four nights in a row
Now call me thus as I wait for you

"Staabash neesh vaas uraaheem bliishneesh vaa"

Now I am ready to enhance your sight
Into the stars if you do it right
See what you will, at first focus much
State your intent of what should be searched
Thus I'll reveal what I may to you
For only integrity's bidding do I do

Spell for Sacred Object 2: A Magical Wand

Ueshm huum uruu veesh vaarm hesheen
Susaavii baa eeshvaa kluu huem
Staavaa oosheen baa klii staa vaa
Viish traa bii iee klee vaa staa muunim

Wait till a storm splits the sky
After carrying it with you on your person 10 days
Then point at the lightening, the rod in your hand
Speak three times these words and commands

"Braaveesh heespaa bluush pareem
Suu vaa neesh braa vuu plaa veem
Staashmeesh rush vaa saarvaa heem"

Then return the wand to the earth
Bury it deep in earth's womb to give birth
To the magic that slumbers deep in its soul
After four days it's retrieved from its hole

Veez uuz beesh paa ruu vee staa oosh vaarim
Klersh mii eesh staa ufraahim valavaash
Nuush baash rush vaaroom wa mish oosh vaash vaa baa

Bring it forth and place it in a stone ring to lie
While you circle to right around the outside three times
Then to the left five times more
Then say these words and your magic's secure

"Gaash veesh staa voorim puureem huurim staa
Meeshoos veeshawaa truunim kluush uur teshaa
Ni-eesh vrush waruum, Ni-eesh oonim staa
Klee-eesh hurus vees nuu vee barshaa"

Spell for Sacred Object 3: Creating a Memory Box

Voosh vees aasavaam Hoos hush hesh
Splee ree traa oosmbee Vaa nuu saa buu esh
Klustaa baa ushvaa ooreem baar nuu seem
Klee es trees nuus vaarn vaa ustree baa uklu

The memory box you keep
Is where memories can sleep
Where when you pull them out again
They can be, as it was, relived again

The box you make, must be by you produced
Only wood or stone in making it use
Find wood that's hard and stone that's soft
While you make it relive happy pasts

Create it well, then with a magical spell
It will hold and replay the bygone days
Say now words when it's complete
Then speak these words in the box to keep

"Bilesheem vii kluuvaaoom virs naastuu bra oo varoom
Stuu-uu staa baa uu vaaeesh nustaa vaa u manuneesh"

As you speak it into its depth
Close it quickly when you've said your spell
Keep it locked and guard it well
Let it sit fourteen days for results

Mish trana baleesh veeshoo siim mee na vaa
Voosh eesh bleesh vaa uusta vaa
Nuu veesh viish staa baa
Oosh nii sush vii stash vaa eesh vru veshvii staarbaa

Then open the box and speak again
The words we give you from the Mer people clans
Three times say it into the box
For four days keep it tightly locked

"Nuspaavim oosh vaash mavim
Oosh praa vaa ustaa oovrim
Pelesh veesh oos vaas vraavim"

Thereafter when a good day has been
Images into it from your third eye beam
Of what has transpired.
Then when you desire once more, when opened the images see

The Shield to Safeguard the Magic of the Mer People

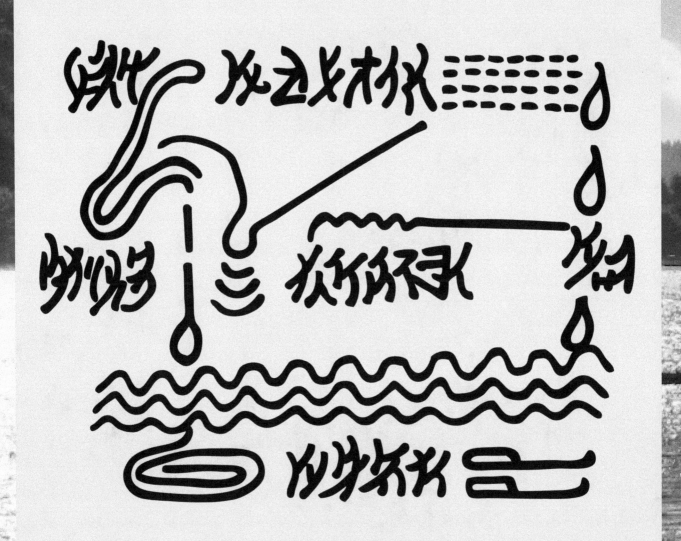

Praa sooo nannang. Ookraa oonee hanannoo.

Magic of the Giants

Introduction to the Giants

There are many references to giants in the Bible. In Genesis 6:4, they are referred to by the name Nephilim, a Hebrew word for giant. In Deuteronomy 2:11, they are referred to as the Anakim and also as the Rephaim. The Rephaim were a pre-Israelite race of giants. The Anakim were a race of giants, descendents of the Nephilim Emim. The following are but a few references provided.

Bible verses that reference Giants

(Genesis 6:4) The Nephilim were on the earth in those days, and also afterward, when the sons of God came in to the daughters of men, and they bore children to them. These were of old, the men of renown.

(Numbers 13:32) So they brought to the people of Israel an evil report of the land which they had spied out, saying "the land through which we have gone, to spy it out, is a land that devours its inhabitants; and all the people that we saw in it are men of great stature."

(Numbers 13:33) And there we saw the Nephilim (the sons of Anak, who come from the Nephilim); and we seemed to ourselves like grasshoppers, and so we seemed to them.

(Deuteronomy 2:10 & 2:11) The Emim formerly lived there, a people great and many, and tall as the Anakim; they are also known as Rephaim, but the Mo`abites call them Emim.

(Samuel 21:16) And Ish'bibe'nob, one of the descendants of the giants, whose spear weighed three hundred shekels of bronze, and who was girded with a new sword, thought to kill David.

(Samuel 21:18) After this there was again war with the Philistines at Gob; then Sib'be`cha`i the Hu`sha`-thite slew Saph, who was one of the descendants of the giants.

(Samuel 21:20) And there was again war at Gath, where there was a man of great stature, who had six fingers on each hand, and six toes on each foot, twenty four in number; and he also was descended from the giants.

(Samuel 21:22) These four were descended from the giants in Gath; and they fell by the hand of David and by the hand of his servants.

The 'Gold Museum' of Lima, Peru has displays of giant skulls and mummies who were thought to be Royalty, according to the clothing and artifacts they had with them when they were discovered. There were photos of two of these mummies taken by Glenn Kimball in 1969. These giants can still be seen by anyone today who visits the museum.

WWW.IAMPRESENCE.COM/SPELLS/GIANTS

Giant Customs, Cultural and Magic Rituals

Giant Ritual:
To Make Actions Beneficial

Through the ages a song is sung
On a single note[8] a single hum

"Bar ba vesbi stanuk ru
Bar ba vesbi pilish stu

Bar ba vesbi glunik sta
Bar ba vesbi ganugs va

Bar ba vesbi spilu mish
Bar ba vesbi sabu vish"

(Translation)
Through my actions create a space
Through my actions make a change
Through my actions let good be done
Through my actions benefit everyone

Through my actions make alive
Through my actions fulfill good desires

Make a circle of candlelight
Make it close from left to right
Then you sing the song again
As you walk around within

Then again you circle the ring
While oil of orange you sprinkle within
This signals that none may enter in
That magical rituals will now begin
Then you say the words out loud:

"Ich bu anik bela suba ha
Vilink sachva balunk ska
Birtl es va granug sta
Mich nut vlsk dra u fra va"

8. The note is G.

134

These words a call to the Giants are
To summon their magic wherever you are
Now begin to focus desire
A focus these words will surely inspire

"Bar ba vesbi stanuk ru
Bar ba vesbi pilish stu

Bar ba vesbi glunik sta
Bar ba vesbi ganugs va

Bar ba vesbi spilu mish
Bar ba vesbi sabu vish

Valvechklut harsh barbarak
Glikstrik nan hurt vartlvak

Blubl us vi van an nat
Krig blik sar vu ninirk stu vechs vi sat"

Now it's time for you to do
The rituals we share with you

Giant Customs Ritual 1:
To Restore True Love

Gel babla subla hit virsk nit islklut
Stablba hesh va vis ba kletnat sku varklvthesh
Kluglat sibl va bra sa ba ru
Yla stra ba ruk mit bilshbavanug us

The ritual we give true love to restore
To help feelings flow, to be free as before
Only to use if love once was there
It only will work if love has been shared

Usefvi kraq unat ish valesvu
Pluag vra ba uvra vilsh bri bra vu

Use now the paint to draw the one's face
Use now the words to say as you paint

"Klugstra mirvash ufba hef
Kelignud eresba uvl bartl hesh
Sut bach ba urasfa vi
Ules va klut
Nangrd bulesva eskvrtlvi
Brubag plavu"

No matter how accurate is your art
As you paint it's the feelings you have in your heart
Say too the words[9] over from finish to start

Vra sit vich vrlshalvi brasba elch varasba
Tubar vi shelsablakut eresh nus vis va ha

Place now the painting in a circle of light
13 candles circle round from left to right
Pronounce it to be a receptive womb
Drawing in love from your loved one soon

9. Those given in the preceeding paragraph.

Then let it lie in its very own room
Where 13 candles shine to banish the gloom
When this is done for fourteen days
Under your mattress it must stay

Giant Customs Ritual 2:
To Keep Your Child Secure

Sut afbalknut echva bilsh havra
Klu stra balach vis tsh ul vris skaluba

And now a ritual for children you have
To keep them secure as though holding your hand

Stau balak virs klaru ma pli
Eglug brvavikstru avru ver
Kiglhit pilich virt balashtra
Kuglvk nin abal ufghlm mir natra

Say these words over a blanket
Wrapped around the child's pillow
Picture with love the child's hand in yours
All the while saying these words

"Branich brstra uref het
Pil ba jurs tra uvra set
Kelech vi nu sti har uvrabat
Kagr usba hirk va stat"

Then picture the child wrapped in its warmth

Trau nk vik baresh vit.
Krech ma nua vers klit
Stu ufba rech vi achvra hat
Klesh ufba uvra vet selshvt bra bat

Whenever you want to, whenever there's cause
As you see in your mind the child now secure
Whisper these words of magic so pure

"Branich brstra uref het
Pil ba jurs tra uvra set
Kelech vi nu sti har uvrabat
Kagr usba hirk va stat"

Photo of Giant taken in a Toronto class.

Giant Customs Ritual 3:
To Clear Ties with Departed Loved Ones

Mir nach ves brtl klsvi vas
Brrsta prvik hili braf bak sta
Blichvr sirtl ka balag nut
Vilsh sat bl kravanug surtl vrut

To clear ties with loved ones who are no longer near
To purify space when vacated by those you hold dear
This is the ritual that sends them along
Free from ties or even bindings strong

Take a container of silver - it must be pure
Place it within a stream's water clear
Let it rest in the water running fast
For a while only, is as long as it lasts

This must be done when you awake
Along to the stream an object you take
Of the loved one departed, the one you hold dear
Remove the container filled with water clear

Place the object now on the bottom[10] to rest
Carry the bowl to the loved one's room
Let it sit; five days are best
When completed to the stream yet again

Release the water with object into the stream
Say three times these words and the one is released

"Beres plavi hubl hik
Usbaa aavra viristik."

10. Of the cup or bowl.

Giant Customs Ritual 4: To Find Your Mate

Svarvi hrtl elek vi
Stabra usl stalech vi
Mir ne us vis btl us va vaa
Klhspt blublag staa

Finding your mate can easy be
Use this ritual and you will see
The mate of your choice attracted to you
The ritual will call one who'll want you too
Write now these words that you may recall
What to use in this ritual

Honey you'll use with vinegar mixed
Red pepper, too, sprinkled on top
Make a circle of stones on a hill
Round to the right sprinkle that which you mixed
Now walk once around saying these words

"Parchva iles vis ba ruk
Klagnk veres varasta vruk
Bilich hishpa krtl het
Nusbi elech satru vit"

Enclosed now you sit with fire and wood
Each quality wanted, well understood
Burn a stick with each quality seen
Calling it forth in the partner to be
Wait 'till the fire has burned itself out
Arise with outstretched arms and these words shout

"Kerech ni va vilsh vabrag bilisnik
Kelsh pirim esta vea asva kluvivanik
Esvaa urech vish balak nug
Stala barfru ba vit elskla barstug"

This will deliver your love to you
In case they're not ready, repeat every full moon

Giant Culture Ritual 1:
To Grow Seeds

To make the seeds grow when the seasons are right
Be sure to sow them when all are asleep
Then this ritual do three times

Birch nit sil varasba klg prfnit
Ush baa hut savranit kelesh vra vras
Prug nat bars vit klava ustra
Nug hit bil achvaa bak sklu avastraa

From each direction take some sand
In the middle of your garden, and place in your hand
Mix it together with water from your well
Into a paste that you spread on your skin
Now dance in circles while saying the chant
Let your feet move wherever they want

"Baresh Klar mis pa tawa
Huf elxgri
Sutbat bla ufbavi
Exbrank stee
Glunik a strafbaha
Varis vi akvavi
Mirat vranavis
Kuch stara vri vrach
Us bavervihet
Stu banik vra hespavat
Elik starug"

Dance with arms like wings to the sky
Dance till you clear all of your mind
Dance till forgetfulness takes hold of you
Then this ritual will do what it must do

Giant Culture Ritual 2: To Keep You Warm

Through snow and rain
You won't complain
The heat this brings
Will keep you warm

"Panig hesh va esbuch brak
Pilig brskblaf heres vi blach
Stubach bi kelsh usabaruk
Mirklesblk varanos ustaa varastik"

With each saying of these words
Weave a face of warmth into place
Picture a loved one's warm embrace
With each saying a blanket is woven into place[11]

Resist not the cold, let it go through
Breathe warmth into the blanket woven for you
Each out-breath blows in, memories you hold
Each thread you weave keeps out the cold

11. Not a physical blanket, but one you create in the etheric realms that can be called upon as needed to warm you.

Giant Culture Ritual 3:
For Tasty Food

To help food taste good, a pyramid build
Of perfect proportions, of glass and gold
But mark each side with a vertical line
Or embalm it will, instead of refine
Over your food that's stored within
Say these words to the food within

"Belbash hishvek stuarag
Nunbag keleg stuavat
Breneg sitvu staubek
Ilesh vil staba urug naneg"

Thank the food that lies within
For the joy to come, for the life that was given

Giant Culture Ritual 4:
To Gain Life Force from Clothes

Clothes can bring life force or clothes can bring none
Clothes will bring strength when rituals are done
Now let me tell you, now let it be known
Bring strength to your life through that which is shown

The clothes must be made with utmost care
When made with love, strength will be there
When you receive them, put them in Sun
Let the wind stroke them, let rain comb each one

Then let them dry in the Sun's pure light
Saying these words to make them feel right

"Buresachna hiosu hesh Kelug bastra
Usit vanatesh"

The Writings of the Giants 1

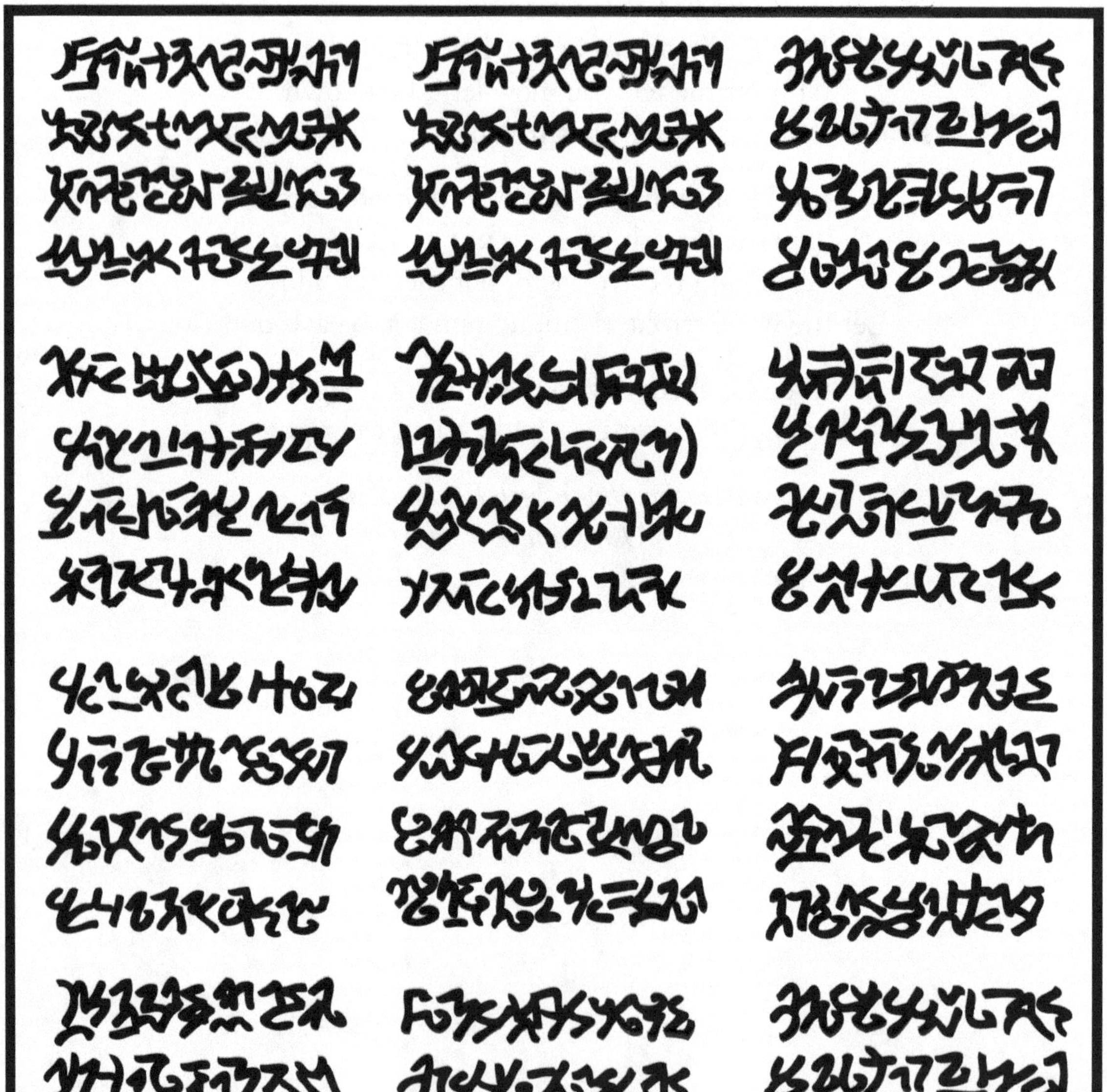

The Writings of the Giants 2

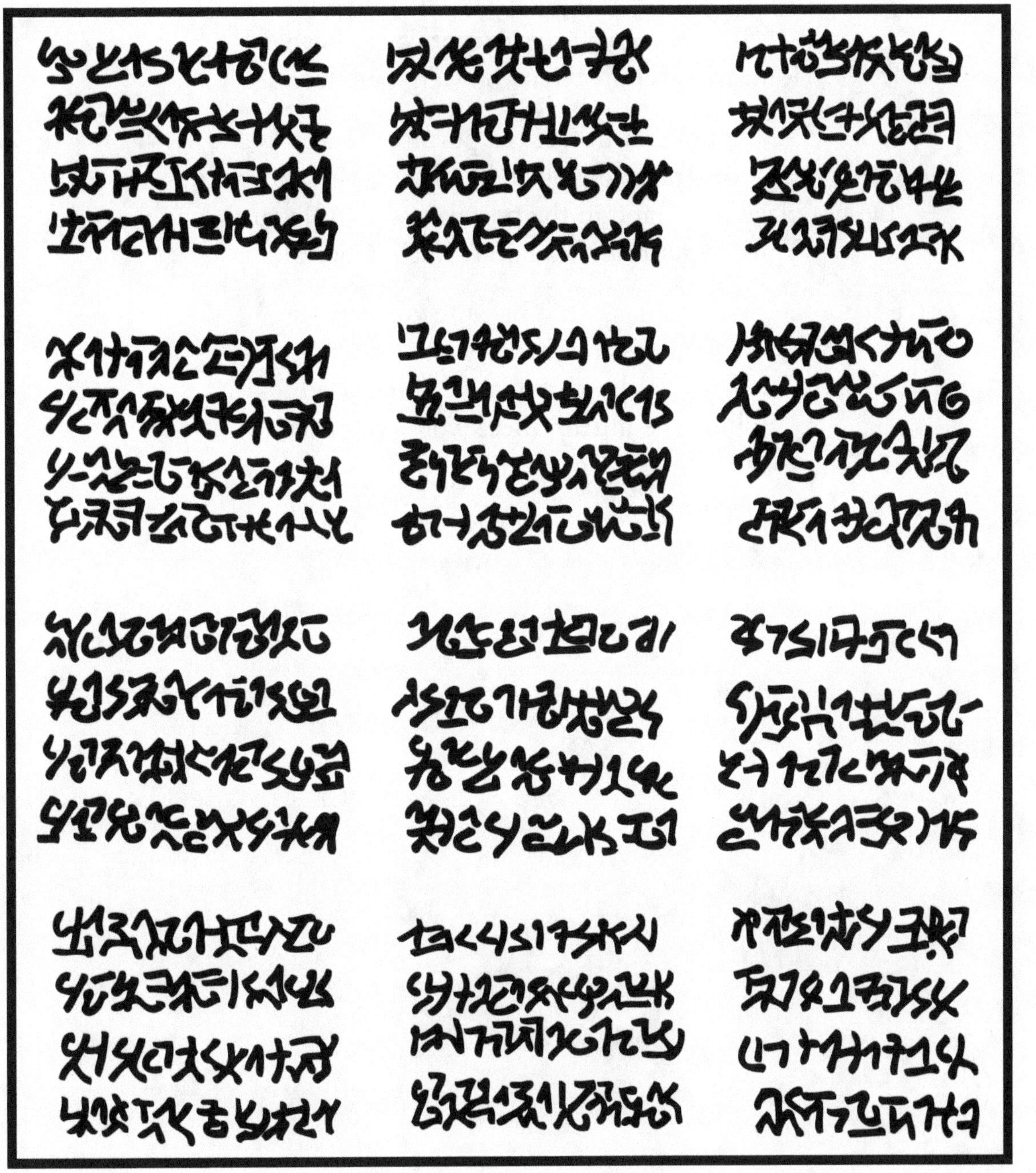

Giant Magic Ritual 1:
For Mirrors

The mirror you see is not what it seems
The mirror you see is what you believe
Reflection is only what you were taught to see

A mirror in fact is a portal of blue
With unprogrammed vision blue swirls there for you
Do not place your hand in the portal; it will pull you through
You can get lost if you don't know what to do

But if you can exit because you can see
Others can enter as well as leave
To close the portal garlic you'll need
Rub on the mirror, these words you speak

*"Klishbraag hufl su vetvi uset
Biliksgrignit urit man ba uruset"*

Giant Magic Ritual 2:
To Gather Magic

To gather the magic of each ritual you do
We shall give a secret this day to you
Gather the ashes of fires you build
Use them to place under your bed
As you sleep the bygone rituals

Shall support and sustain
Giving you energy 'till you sleep again
The way to release their gift to you
Is to speak over the ashes these words of truth

"Kelspa susutvi Balsh bla klanug staa
Uf af vra banavik bluvik helsh braak vaa
Sufl efl varrel het Bli u bach baar klk vra hesh
Buch u sa ba vusha hut gilklit hesvaa nin hurset"

Giant Magic Ritual 3:
To Find Your Sigil

Afvra hus ba va nesh kluag
Stabl urvesvi klaster
Uberik bilchvi u aa nu staarvi
Kirs haberach baalich selve vaa
Hersh vaa ursblt kelesvaa

Here's the way to strengthn your life
Find the sigil that's yours to write
Like a symbol but not the same
Your personal sigil is like your name

It draws in energy to your life's cause
Place it on power objects that are yours
Write when mind is silenced and still
Let your hand go where it will

The sigil will form as you write
Deep satisfaction knows it is right

Giant Magic Ritual 4:
To Bond a Newborn with the Earth

From the birth comes a cord
Which can strengthen the newborn
In a bag of leather made
Amongst feathers and sand

In a pine tree's shade
Hide the cord and cover it tight
Bury it well – out of sight
Let it rest for several days
Before removed, these words you say

*"If varink natvi kelba staverrut
Kilsh echva nutvi balsk usalvaa"*

To the Earth this babe announced
The bond can now be forged

*"Brstranuk pilsh valelvaa hut
Kaluch baa uvra varshbrut"*

Let loyalty be given, loyalty received
The Earth now knows this babe as friend

The Shield to Safeguard the Magic of the Giants

Esklavu nishpa eres vrinas plahu erekta

Magic of the Lords of Light

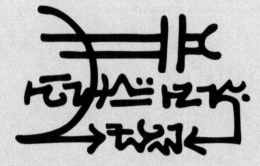

Key 1

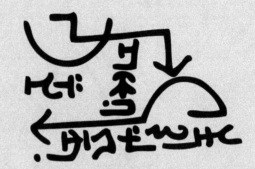

Key 2

Key 3

Understanding More About the Lords of Light

A great miracle one day you will see
When Mother answers the lonely lords' plea
Billions of lords, all of them male,
Shall ask the Mother to create their mates

For eons the workforce of the cosmos they have been
But mates for the lords have never been seen
When Mother this great gift on them bestows
A wave of delight through the cosmos goes

The wives and lords the Mother will praise
With so much energy that the cosmos will raise
And all life will move through a door
To levels the cosmos has never been in before

Sheresach vibresvi haruvistat arsakla minesu
Rustave hirasut miseklech seranersavut
Hirusat erekluhasat misenechvu erasu

The Kingdom of the Lords of Light represents the nervous system of man. In order to graduate to the god kingdom stages, the feminine, frequency component of the nervous system needs to be functional. This allows the inner senses' input to register. The next evolutionary step of supergod requires the merging into one of both components – this will merge the Lords of Light in bliss and happiness with their feminine counterparts.

Kee ee-gach bira ninert sarva
skalegug

The sigil to cleanse the
magnetic portions of mind at rest

What is mind at rest that around the
cosmos lies
An electro-magnetic field around
each being you'll find
Cleanse now the memory from the
magnetic parts of the fields
And in man's behaviour a
difference you'll see

Chavek birashpi menuhak
Ares prihatvava mesetu

The feminine of the Lords dysfunctional became
Holding memories of fear and pain
To the Lords they did complain
Wanting to contribute, thus purpose to gain
To the Holy Mother did they pray

Their prayers were answered upon that day
As one they became with the male
Each contributing in an integrated way
To evolve to godhood possible became
As the purified feminine and masculine blended in grace

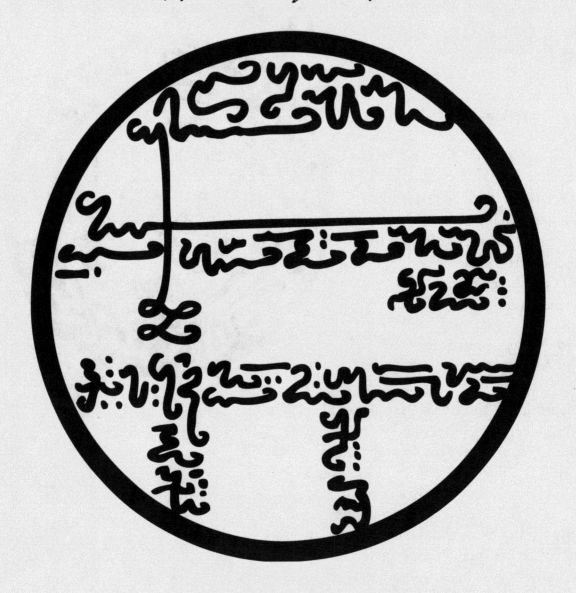

Phases within the God Kingdom

GOD KINGDOM PHASE 2

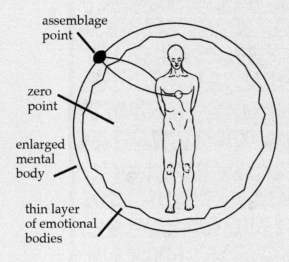

assemblage point

zero point

enlarged mental body

thin layer of emotional bodies

Very few emotions are felt during this phase. Mental body rotates the same as in phase 1.

SUPERGOD KINGDOM PHASE 1

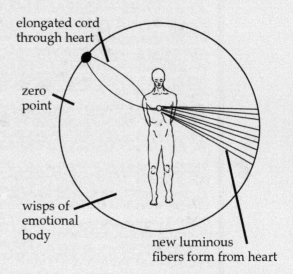

elongated cord through heart

zero point

wisps of emotional body

new luminous fibers form from heart

Fields are 6 times the length of the physical body. Mental body has partial rotations alternating clockwise/counter clockwise.

SUPERGOD KINGDOM PHASE 2

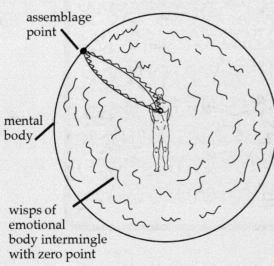

assemblage point

mental body

wisps of emotional body intermingle with zero point

Fields are now 50 times larger. The luminous fibers from previous phase have now thickened the cord.

SUPERGOD KINGDOM PHASE 3

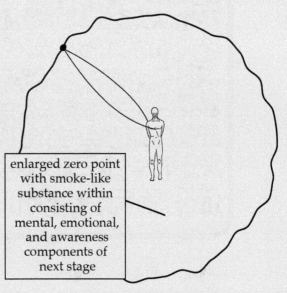

enlarged zero point with smoke-like substance within consisting of mental, emotional, and awareness components of next stage

Fields are 360 times larger. Cord is stretched thin again and solid mental body is gone.

The assemblage point determines what is being observed. The large field around the body is a field of observation. In the supergod kingdom, they function together in an integrated way.

The Lords of Light and the Library of the Dove

The Lords of Light is a very little understood kingdom, embodying the principles of light. In certain instances they are given specific tasks, such as to be the guardians of the magical components found in the magic of the Library of the Dove.

The masculine nature of the magic of the Dove is electrical or masculine. It is for this reason that the Lords of Light, representing a masculine component in the cosmos, are the ones that have become the guardians of this sacred body of information.

The Lords of the Beak of the Dove

Formed from the Sothic Triangle

(+ -)
Suhit-aresta
Lord of Understanding of Movement and Measure

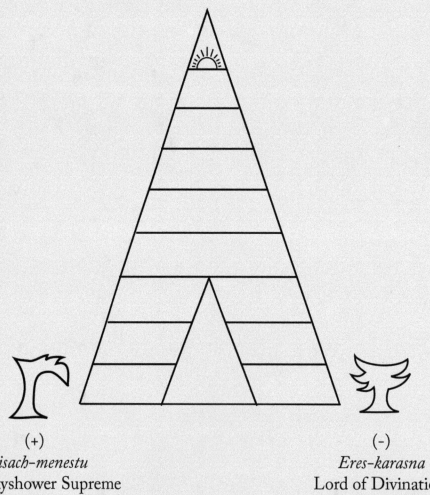

(+)	(-)
Misach-menestu	*Eres-karasna*
The Wayshower Supreme	Lord of Divination,
Guide	The High Priest

The Sothic Triangle of Initiation used by the Order of the White Dove.

The Lords of the Initiations of Man

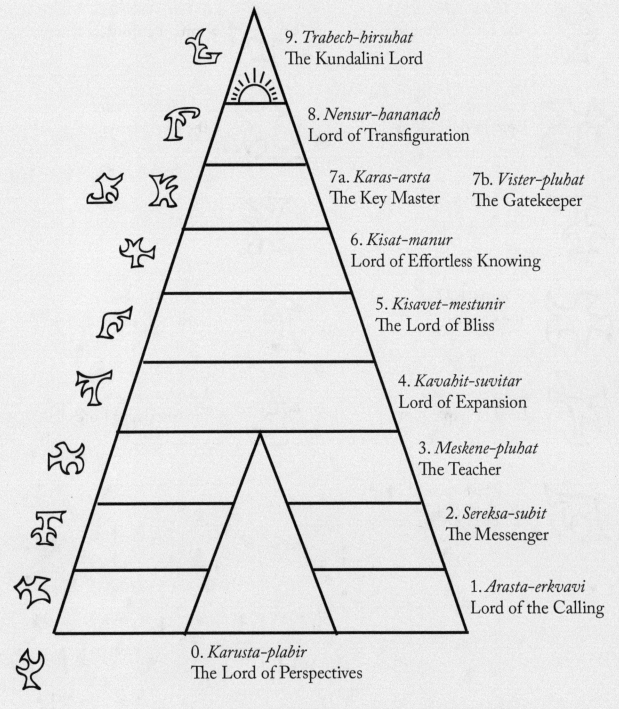

9. *Trabech-hirsuhat*
The Kundalini Lord

8. *Nensur-hananach*
Lord of Transfiguration

7a. *Karas-arsta*
The Key Master

7b. *Vister-pluhat*
The Gatekeeper

6. *Kisat-manur*
Lord of Effortless Knowing

5. *Kisavet-mestunir*
The Lord of Bliss

4. *Kavahit-suvitar*
Lord of Expansion

3. *Meskene-pluhat*
The Teacher

2. *Sereksa-subit*
The Messenger

1. *Arasta-erkvavi*
Lord of the Calling

0. *Karusta-plabir*
The Lord of Perspectives

The two Lords at the seventh level are known as the Lords of the Two Doors.
The Lord that keeps the unworthy from entering the Initiations is Karusta-plabir,
the Lord of Perspectives.

169

The Sigils for the Lords of the Initiations of Man

 0. Ustech-misavet
The Lord of Perspectives

 6. Vitres-piresatvi
Lord of Effortless Knowing

 1. Karsta-ereklus
Lord of the Calling

 7a. Michpe-rusata
The Key Master

 2. Pitrehut-miseta
The Messenger

 7b. Piras-ersata
The Gatekeeper

 3. Arspa-arechvi
The Teacher

 8. Arskle-huvraset
Lord of Transfiguration

 4. Kiresat-husva
Lord of Expansion

 9. Serkla-pereshu
The Kundalini Lord

 5. Urkspa-menesut
The Lord of Bliss

Incantations from the Lords of the Beak of the Dove

Incantation 1:
To Strengthen Other Spells

Archbarut sirklatva eksparut milesant
Kruhabit eksanus natrit selvatur

Call it forth from beyond the abyss
Call in the ancient magic like this
Use these words before each spell
Say them thrice and say them well

Incantation 2:
To Solve a Mystery

Brivatur nanusat herskletklava

I command now the turning of keys
Reveal to me this mystery

Incantation 3:
For Truth to be Revealed

Nachbi piras urstet maneshvi
Hesetrach krivanes sublet bavi

Let perception dawn from the Source of Light
Let truth reveal itself before my sight
This incantation removes all veils
When its words I four times say
From long ago these words prepared
That no illusion from being banished be spared

Incantation 4:
To Remove Negative Emotions or Negativity from Others

Usaranesh

Get thee hence

Incantation 5:
To Call the Names of Sacred Beings

Nanprachvek

I evoke _____ (follow with the name)[12]

12. Only positive beings can be evoked.

Incantation 6:
For Attracting an Immaculate Conception

Brahes mirabach suvesvi
Eskrahut plibasut minanet
Trihas ubaveshbavi manuset

For conception immaculate as well
Use three times the words of this spell
Draw in a spirit high and refined
Into the womb marked with this sign

Sigil for Fertility

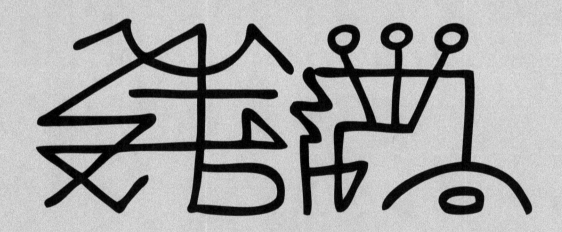

This sigil is used for fertility and is drawn on the womb area of the abdomen.

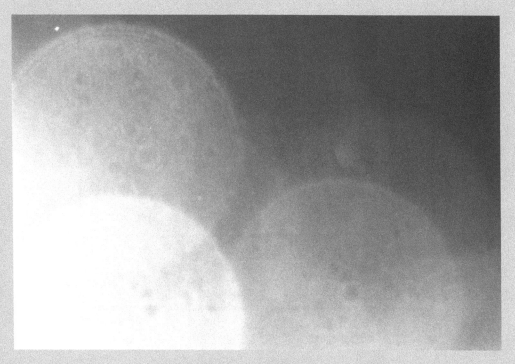

Immaculate babies waiting to be conceived.
Of the 11 masters gathered for the holy ceremony, 5 conceived immaculately.

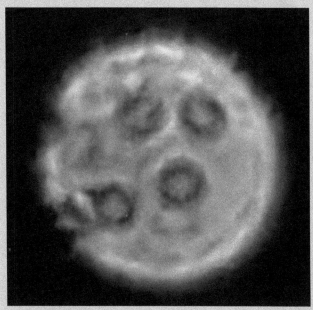

More detailed photo of an immaculate baby.

"I was present on two occasions
when the Seer Almine facilitated
immaculate conceptions. I have seen
the two little boys since then and
remember how they
entered the womb as a bright
blue ball of light. Truly a miracle!"

- Jan, Ohio -

Incantation 7:
To Undo Ill Intent

Shpach barek minhur eshtra baravech
Kerenach sertu esevisbi
Klanech nespa klihur esetretvi

Undo the schemes of ill intent
Let this spell unspin the web
Reverse the energy thus far spent
That blessings flow to me instead

Let plans be hindered one and all
That meant to harm and cause my fall

Incantation 8:
To Shield Innocence

Hirskrahet eset uselvranach
Pranat bilshtre estru ustranet

Surrounded by light innocence stands
A shield to protect against tainted hands
None shall touch the one that bears
The shield of this spell when the sigil is there

Sigil for Incantation 8

To protect innocence, this sigil is visualized into the fields of the one to be shielded.

Incantation 9:
To Obtain Inner Balance

First say this incantation three times.

Mirach vrihaspranut esekle
Harus senet avrubachvi
Hirsatrer eseruch mistral nevti

From discordant energies of others nearby
In an egg of light let me hide
The seven directions gathered around
When the sigil of this spell in my fields are found
Then call in the seven directions.

1) *Urstrabi*	Within
2) *Mitravu*	Below
3) *Arekna*	Above
4) *Ruksebi*	North
5) *Arusba*	East
6) *Sesklanu*	West
7) *Ekprahur*	South

Sigil for Incantation 9

*This sigil can be drawn in shoes, on skin or visualized in
one's fields to keep a sacred space in dense surroundings.*

The Head of the Dove
The Lords of the Seven Directions

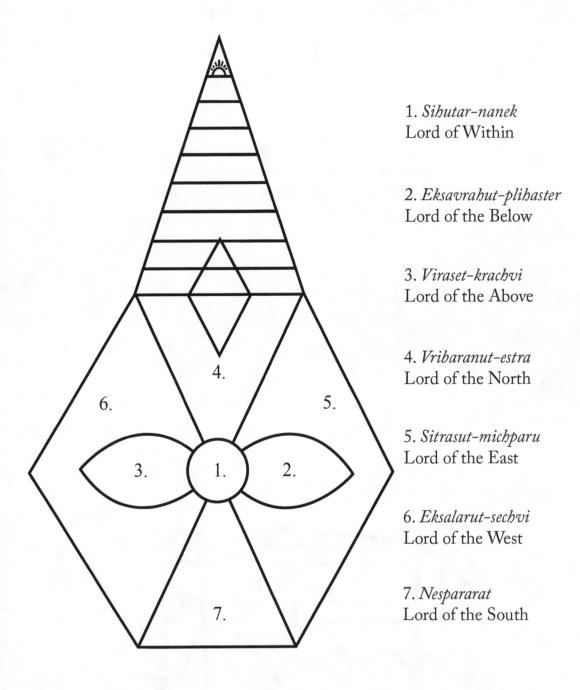

1. *Sihutar-nanek*
Lord of Within

2. *Eksavrahut-plihaster*
Lord of the Below

3. *Viraset-krachvi*
Lord of the Above

4. *Vribaranut-estra*
Lord of the North

5. *Sitrasut-michparu*
Lord of the East

6. *Eksalarut-sechvi*
Lord of the West

7. *Nespararat*
Lord of the South

The Lords of the Seven Directions are the archetypes of the directions.
The Mother Goddess holds the energies of the seven directions.

Lords for the Functions of Mind
(as found in different parts of the brain)

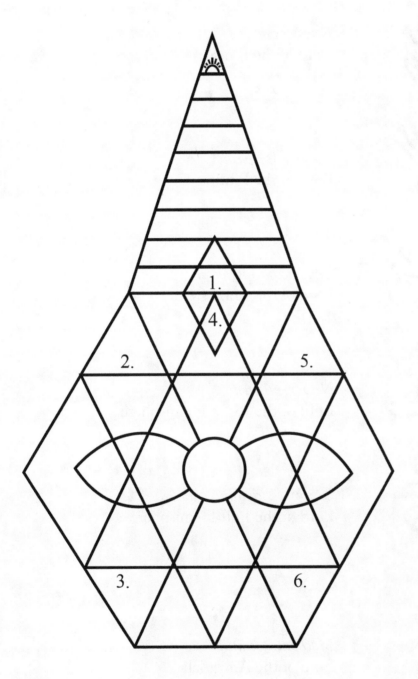

1. *Nesklararat*
Lord of the Pituitary

2. *Keshvelavi*
Lord of the Amygdala

3. *Akvarskurat*
Lord of the
Left Hemisphere

4. *Mensuhavi*
Lord of the Pineal

5. *Kivererut*
Lord of the Brain Stem

6. *Piherestat*
Lord of the
Right Hemisphere

There are the six Lords that govern the
functions of mind found within the head of the Dove.

Sigils of the Six Lords
for the Center of the Dove's Head

Etreva–suklesvi
Lord of the Pineal

Nusenat–pribasut
Lord of the Pituitary

Truherechbi–esklavat
Lord of the Brain stem

Nespar–misenet
Lord of the Right Hemisphere

Uspekva–suvahit
Lord of the Left Hemisphere

Machpatu–sesanit
Lord of the Amygdala

Incantations from
the Lords of the
Head of the Dove

Incantation 1:
To Speak the Ancient Languages

Ursanach betrut birak esevechvi
Nensech skrihutret esabi mikluvesh

Release to me the ancient tongues
Let me speak a powerful and sacred one
Let me know the meaning of the words
Let me translate the holy language heard

Incantation 2:
To Cultivate Telepathy

Nutrahek siklu vrisevas

Open the door for telepathy's gift
To communicate to kingdoms through the use of it
Let me hear in words I can understand
Transmissions from the kingdoms to the world of man

Incantation 3:
To Increase the Accuracy of Divination

Mechpahur silvaset mishunech

Speak these words[13] to a divining device
Truth it must tell, it cannot then lie
No mind can interfere not even your own
The answers it gives shall be truth alone

Incantation 4:
To Write Ancient Glyphs

Spraruk belspavit estranut
Pirtravet reksavi usbrach beneshvi

Seven times shall these words be said
To awaken the language of symbols within the head
Written languages and sigils shall reveal themselves
To translate and write and interpret them well

---

13. They need to be said five times.

Incantation 5:
For Remote Viewing

Neksa briseruch plihavas ninserat

To view remotely, this spell will aid
By impeccability must all decisions be made
The use of these words will give you sight
Into other locations, if you have the right

Incantation 6:
To Remember Past Lives

Beresh nasvi skivaklut

These words seven times repeat
If it is memories you wish to retrieve
Then sit in silence in a circle of myrrh
Ancient memories within you will stir

The Eleven Lords of the Dove's Torso

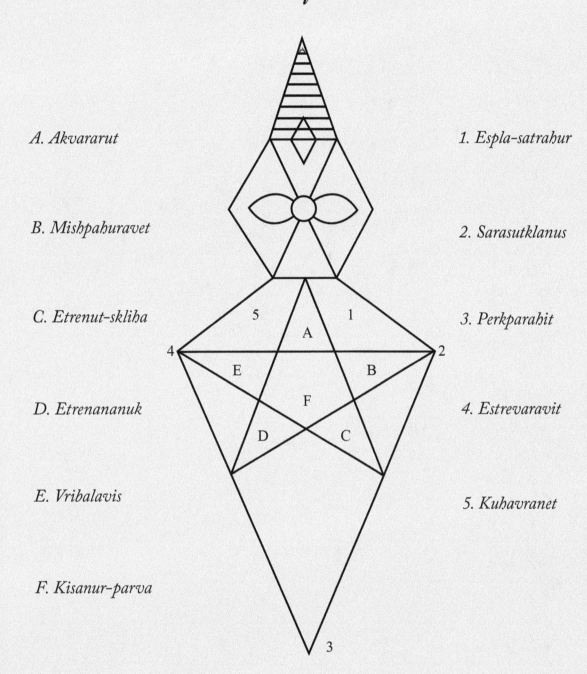

A. Akvararut

B. Mishpahuravet

C. Etrenut-skliha

D. Etrenananuk

E. Vribalavis

F. Kisanur-parva

1. Espla-satrahur

2. Sarasutklanus

3. Perkparahit

4. Estrevaravit

5. Kuhavranet

The eleven Lords that form the torso of the Dove are also a map of the heart. The map of the heart consists of two interlocking five-pointed stars, intersecting at 90° angles.

The Sigils for the Eleven Lords of the Dove's Torso

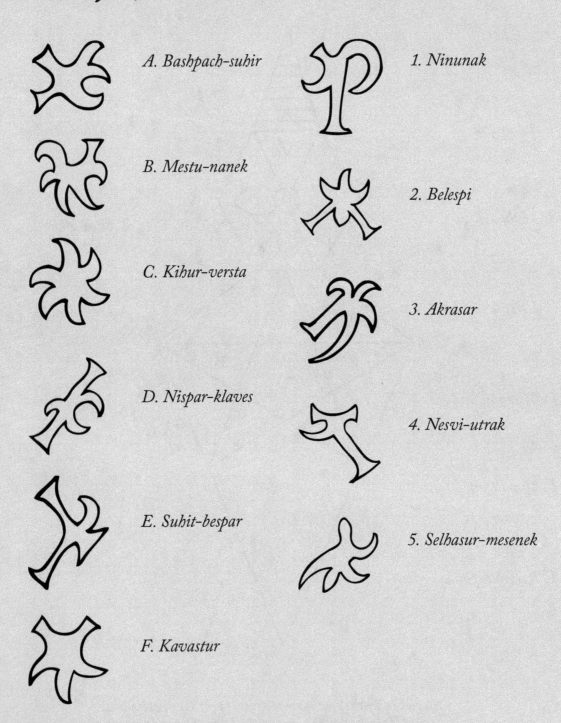

A. Bashpach–suhir

B. Mestu–nanek

C. Kihur–versta

D. Nispar–klaves

E. Suhit–bespar

F. Kavastur

1. Ninunak

2. Belespi

3. Akrasar

4. Nesvi–utrak

5. Selhasur–mesenek

Incantations from the Lords of the Torso of the Dove

Incantation 1:
To Fulfill a Desire

Stabavech kersanut harasvi
Mishetech uskret nanut
Bisel anuch mishet aranu

Fill the space I did create
Where the need exists, fill the space
Four times over the words I will say
As I envision how the need fulfilled will stay

Where there is lack, let plenty be
Fulfill what I want in the way I see
Naught of the need must remain
Let abundance from the ether flow this way

Incantation 2:
To Enhance Well-being

Bravech satsatva unasvi harastu
Mishet aras minuvesvi aras
Krihusat balachsta mines uretkrava

Let comfort surround the faces I envision
Fill their hearts with peace and well-being
Bring to their mind visions of hope
In times of sadness help them cope

Keeping their faces firm in my mind
The magical words I now repeat thrice

Incantation 3:
To Activate Runes

Mechpa nuserat ilstrechvi
Sihut treve elespa nuserak
Kerhutra sibarut menserat usbi

Potent the runes in my hand I hold
For me only let their truth be told
Three days at noon when the sun is high
The words I will speak to bring forth their light

High in the sky like a golden ring
The sun will shine and the Dove will bring
Power to these runes by the words I say
Ready they are after three days

Incantation 4:
To See the Future Results of Options

Sihanet pluhanesh vrebar
Usekret nenserat ustrevar
Sirch uvasvi prahit nunastet
Kiranasvi bersarut ekrevet

Crystal clear the future reveal
Show me the options before they're here
Let me see clearly my choices' results
Deep do I reach into the occult

These words I speak and repeat them thrice
Then in meditation, before my eyes
Doors shall I see, to me they will appear
Open doors of choices, your futures to reveal

Then as I surrender to that which could be
As in meditation I stay till I see
What the future holds for what I choose
That in wisdom these insights I may use

Incantation 5:
To Keep What is Yours

Manech bruhat stravilesvi
Sektuvut stabahech silvutret
Nenserat skrubanit elskla stubavich
Briharsanut estrabil skruventvi

Claim what is yours, don't hesitate
Take what's your right before it's too late
But know in your heart that this spell is used
Only for that which is yours and you could lose

These words say out loud while in your mind
You see what is yours returned to your side
Embrace it as though it is complete
Let joy fill your heart for accomplishing this feat

Incantation 6:
To Clear the Mind

Saavech biraspi melakrut nenachvi
Subatu pliheresh esanuch viravat
Stuhit melsanur esevech ublavi

Clear your mind of confusion's cause
That clarity returns say these words
Whether confusion results from an external source
Or whether from distorted emotions that are yours

As you say these words you must feel
A wave of energy originating from the pineal
Let it travel from head to feet
Three times as this incantation you repeat

Incantation 7:
To Accumulate Wealth

Sakanut meretach blubarech eskrut harsava
Pelhur kevana enuch brivasbi
Spenhar nursetvi kranas binatur

Accumulate great wealth with these words you must say
But say them you must each day without fail
Write them in sigils of the ancient way
In the place where you keep your money to stay

Try and remember at least ninety days
Not to forget these words to say

Sigil to Create an Abundant Flow of Resources

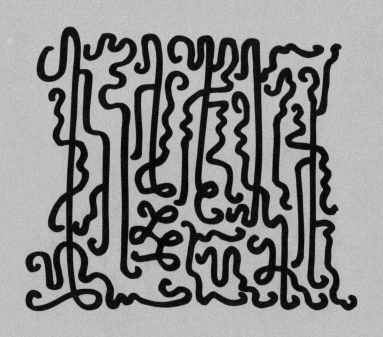

Incantation 8:
To Boost Personal Power

Manech pirabi skelevut
Vastrech brivesh arsanat

Personal power benefits all
With this spell power is called
Pure are the motives that will make it come
But it must be used for the good of all, not just the one

Cry out these words to the Mother's heart
For now a deep secret we will impart
All power that is, comes from one Source
From the physical heart of the Mother it comes forth

Ever-generating that which is needed
The power and energy is never depleted
By Mother's heart is all life sustained
Her heart as the power Source of all life remains

Know this and call with the might of your words
And the power you need shall be yours.

Sigil for Self-empowerment

Incantation 9:
To Clear Buildings of Distortion

Savret mesanuch huvrasbi
Eskrahit sekla subravit menenus
Selvehit kerenash usut manus
Presbar sikrat birespi

Clean with these words buildings and homes
Where others have caused distorted tones
Where thoughts of distortion were before
Let purity once more be restored

Say then four times to the south, west, east and north
Then three times more let these words come forth
To the above and below, the ceiling and floor
Then to the center where you stand, to the within you must call

The words you repeat in every room
If you can; above the ceiling and below the floor too
Envision as you do, a violet light
Send it with your words to make the room bright

Almine Blessing a Student.

Almine Blessing a Student.

200

Incantation 10:
To Awaken Kundalini

Braavech ninasat urespi akra
Brivabesh harusak ekresh mananuch
Sechvet kru-anas sevichva minestra
Su-utrech prahuch minsech hurunas
Klavech vilsavat helesta

To awaken the serpent at the base of the spine
To raise the energy that there reclines
Say these words sexual energy to release
But not just sexuality will it increase

Procreative power releases magic to you
All other spells better you will do
If stagnation occurs at the base of the spine
Manifestation in Mastery also declines

Before – The Magic
of the Red and
White Serpent

The Red and White Serpents represent
the positive (masculine) and negative
(feminine) aspects of Kundalini White
Magic – the third body of white magic
restored to humanity.

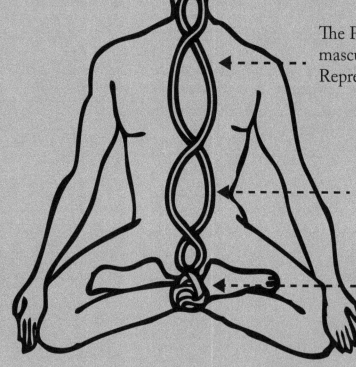

The Pingala – the right, red
masculine channel of energy:
Represented by the Red Serpent.

The Ida – the left, white
feminine channel of
energy: Represented by
the White Serpent.

The Kundalini lies
coiled at the base of
the spine.

Increased Consciousness
Before and After

After – The Magic
of the One Serpent

The neutral power of the
one serpent was born in
November 2007 when
Mother healed a rift
in the fabric of
the time/space
continuum.

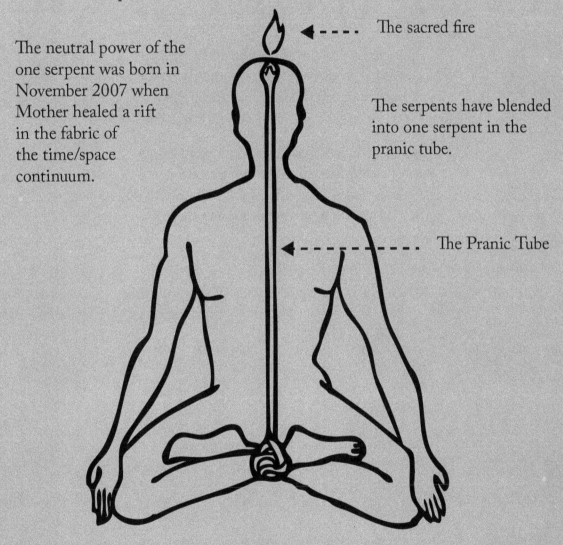

The sacred fire

The serpents have blended
into one serpent in the
pranic tube.

The Pranic Tube

*Note: See "The Sacred Breaths of Arasatma," for techniques to straighten
and use the extended pranic tube that lies coiled at the base of the spine*

Incantation 11:
To Enter the Hall of Destiny

Blavech birshparet masanach uvetvi
Kresva spihuraret esbech prihusut
Eksarut spirahut misurarech rekna vresavi

In ancient libraries your destiny awaits
The destiny of today by tomorrow will change
A library there, those changes reflects
For tomorrow's destiny you by the moment affect

I give you the key and the sacred words too
Access to this library they will give to you
Say the words twice and in meditation you will see
A door of gold in the White Dove's libraries

There you place the key that I give
In the door's inscription where there's a missing piece
The door will then open and you will find within
A crystal that glows as though beckoning

It is destiny beckoning for you to discover
But find only yours, not that of another
Each day you may travel to seek out your own
But the destiny of others may not be known

If this warning by you is mocked
The golden door behind you then will be locked
Speak into the crystal your name three times
Then follow your words with this sacred rhyme

Peranak herstanut isevech mirablut
Peverskla mesenuch hernesat urubluch
Pri-utret mesnavar trihanes usklebar

After you have gazed into the crystal that glows
Your destiny that day you will clearly know
The way you return is the same way you came
Say the same sacred words, but now three times you must say

The incantation that brought you to these sacred doors
The same words you spoke twice before
Now when spoken thrice takes you home
Your life's contribution to the whole you will know

The Key to the Hall of Destiny
in the Libraries of the Dove

Around the door there are 13 discs.
One of the discs has no design on it. This key goes there.

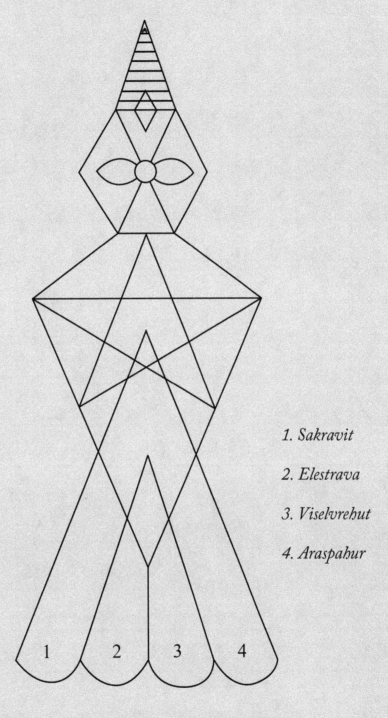

1. Sakravit

2. Elestrava

3. Viselvrehut

4. Araspahur

The nature of these Lords represent flow and fluidity.

Incantations from the Lords of the Tail of the Dove

Ritual 1:
To Create the Fountain of Youth

Kusut ruktrani-baravit eskra
Nachvit elsahur ekrenit pihes trinasur

There are spirals in water that when they are used
Can restore over time the bloom of youth
The codes of the spirals have long been sought
In holy water by an Earthly prince held

But the secrets of the spirals keeping throughout all time
The water fresh he could not find
Mother the spirals removed to the Angel Goddess Number One
That she through fifty angels can give them to some

Those who call these sacred words
Upon whose tongue the angel names are heard
The water in a vessel by them prepared
As pure as can be found and poured through the air

Note: The container should be clear or blue. The water should be poured to aerate it.

Angel Names Given by the Mother for the Fountain of Youth

Skanur

Vribes

Alesklar

Niskavir

Uhutpranis

Arsublit

Krusnachpar

Sekmetur

Ritual 2:
To Balance Gravitation with Levitation

Uprihata skruvivaves utrechmanas elvichve
Plibrabus nismabranit kilsatrer subaha

Gravitation balanced with levitation must be
For not only aging but decay to cease
One of the sacred creational powers of life
Mastering levitation stops the ravages of time

Temples most sacred that last from age to age
Overcome with levitation the signs of decay
Envision yourself or the building in which you stay
Existing a few inches above the ground while sacred words you say

Angels there are whose names you must call
But say first the sacred words before
See yourself and your house fill with light
Feel yourself become light as a feather in flight

Angels to Balance Gravitation with Levitation

Kaavanash

Esbamirachvi

Lisaletvravi

Kipritparusna

Suvechvarstu

Graneshmesenut

Skriblibrahut

Eseterbravish

Ritual 3:
To Communicate with the Spirit World

Kravek vrishanut brechspavi urakve
Kresatu balustra mesark nanutvi
Branush sperchpa krisvanit
Lukspavi prespatur kiritsta

Call the name of the departed one
While envisioning his face as though he is young
The words you speak a tunnel will open
The words must seven times be spoken

Angels there are that will search far and near
To find the departed one you hold dear
If not rebirthed or in a place where he prepares
To re-enter life when a new incarnation is there

If it is possible for him to come
They shall surely find the departed one
Then must you be very still to hear
When finally the loved one speaks in your ear

If you do not succeed at first
Try many more times, you must persist
For sometimes someone is sent on a task
Which they must finish before they can respond at last

The Angels to Find a Departed Loved One

Iktararus

Kinansabrut

Melenerush

Lavenik

Kurustan

Mesebichvi

Silbarahus

Verknavis

Ritual 4:
Ritual of Resurrection

Sakvanut krenit arsta pereklivanek
Rukmerestut anas pliharavek brihustar
Ersat mishtruvanek ekret nanut sibelha
Saksanoch utret maravech

Use these words to resurrect that which almost has died
Whether your heart's desire or a very sick child
Speak these words before the embers grow cold
While yet a spark remains, life it still holds

Call upon angels mighty and pure
Call upon angels if you feel sure
That life resurrected will serve the highest good
Then they will respond if truly they should

Use it fearlessly, you may be bold
For these sacred rituals you need not withhold
They cannot bring that which will bring someone ill
For they serve only the Mother's will

The Angels that Bring Resurrection

Harutna

Mirsblahur

Seksavit

Retbluhestar

Kalesatva-prahir

Nenstukbrahir

Arsatmarve

Plubahus

The Lords of the Wings of the Dove

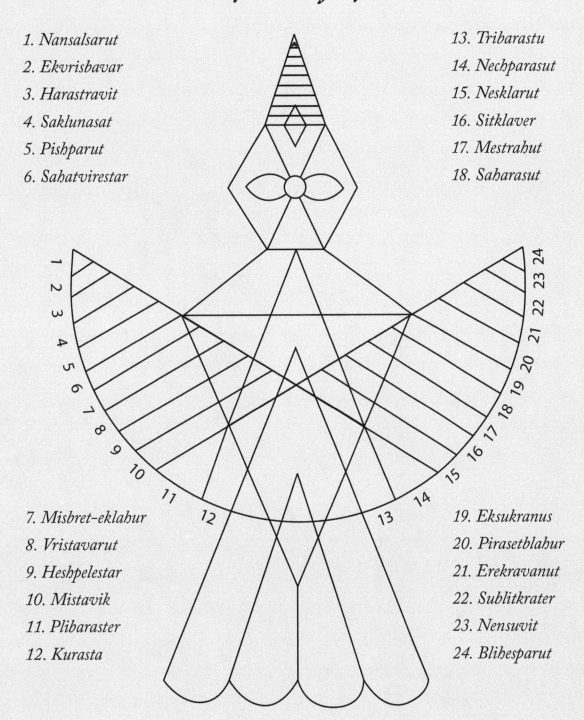

1. Nansalsarut
2. Ekvrisbavar
3. Harastravit
4. Saklunasat
5. Pishparut
6. Sahatvirestar

13. Tribarastu
14. Nechparasut
15. Nesklarut
16. Sitklaver
17. Mestrahut
18. Saharasut

7. Misbret–eklahur
8. Vristavarut
9. Heshpelestar
10. Mistavik
11. Plibaraster
12. Kurasta

19. Eksukranus
20. Pirasetblahur
21. Erekravanut
22. Sublitkrater
23. Nensuvit
24. Blihesparut

The Windows of Wisdom from the Lords of the Tail of the Dove

Window 1:
Prosperity

Kresna priharastekvi
Ersuk plaket mishtrach nadok
Kresdanavit vroch bares arsanut

A dragon's prosperity comes from his tail
This energy you must use to prosper and prevail
You have a tailbone with energy like ours
Now you must learn to harness its power

Draw from this power's resting place
The violet fire with every breath you take
See yourself draw it aloft to the heart
Send it out with any money you impart

Call for prosperity, say then these words
As you spend money though they be unheard
In the tongue of the Mother whom we serve
We give you prosperity's magic words

Prahut sitrechvi aras nusklahur
Esenech sinet aruk peresta
Klies-raktu ersabi kravech harsata ruksavi

Window 2:
Embarkation

Stera-uklahit herestakvi usvabrach
Kretnut usablat perenachvi
Tre-uharanik stihach plehasvi etrebak

When on a journey you embark
When you set out on a venture and wish to make your mark
Create a journey where every step counts
Where along the way deep satisfaction mounts

Around yourself envision a cocoon that with a pink-purple light glows
Carry it with you wherever you go
With these words infuse it with a special trait
To attract to you all that is good, that on your journey awaits

See it as keeping the unwelcome at bay
No discomfort may in your sacred space stay
The cocoon, like a vehicle of grace, its role fulfills
Travelling with you wherever you will

Window 3:
Opportunity

Uskanit sebahur pitrinet
Berat urnis skelechvi
Raktu mashanech sehus asatra
Kelbaruk meshunach sakva

From the palms of your hands a spider web throw
Around the circumstances your mind's eye will show
Be very careful, this you must know
The web must never around people go

See in your mind the way you would live
Then in your mind's eye a spider web weave
Cast now around the image you see
The web and pull in that which shall be

Do this often let more details grow
The more you envision the more it is so

Window 4:
For Infusing Standing Waveforms

Brihashpava nenuk subavi eskra hunechvi
Mishite prahut subahit eskranus eselvravi

When one is ill or a child is born
A dragon ritual is then performed
The same can be done to help infuse
An object with light and magic to use

To understand how this is done
We now explain what takes place between everyone
When two beings stand face-to-face
A few body lengths apart, whatever the race

They strongly send each other love they feel
A waveform is formed in between
When strong enough, a new creation forms
Combined from their feelings a waveform is born

To focus the waveform two crystals are used
They focus the waveform, which is else diffused
One has a point that downward will face
This one above the child or ill one place

The other's point must face to above
Place it below what you will fill with love
Any emotion can be this way infused
But it's stronger in groups when the same emotion's used

This works very well in sacred objects too
But with the words you are given, begin what you do
The words instruct that the emotion you choose
Will stay wherever it is placed by you

Creating a Standing Waveform

An energy field, or waveform is formed as the combined emotional qualities of those creating it.

A waveform is created.

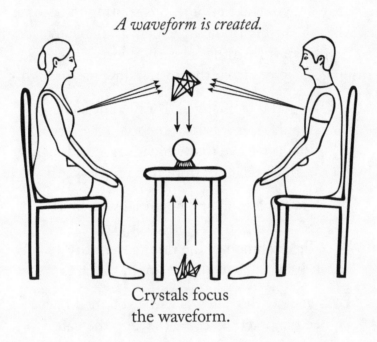

Crystals focus
the waveform.

A crystal ball is infused with healing power by sending healing at one another.

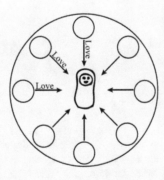

People seated around an infant infuse love into it by sending it at the person seated opposite. The incantation helps it stay. A small crystal placed on top and one below the infant focuses the newly created waveform.

Window 5:
Inspiration

Abek prihata suvetmanu pilistar
Kritvramur nitpave tisblakut

Where are possibilities of things waiting to become
Where lies the inspiration for the new available to everyone
From the Mother's heart, a portal it is
Inspiration comes from the portal, flowing through it

The portal of change it is called by some
For not only does it bring potential for everyone
But as we live that which is received
Our DNA changes from this priceless gift

Thus inspiration and potential well lived
Bring to all a priceless gift
The evolution of life results from this
It brings new reality changing what is

As you say these words while you meditate
See the potential come through the gate
Invite with the incantation's tones
That you be entered by potential's flow

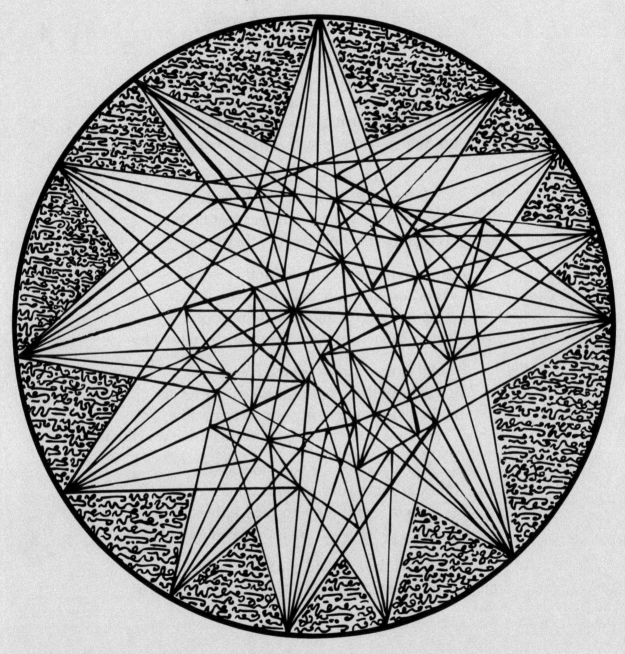

*The frequency of the Mother Goddess's partial expression of a strand of DNA is the result
of a combination of all 96 pure frequencies. The meaning is: Spontaneous Innovative Creation.*

Window 6:
Fluidity

Ratvi sitranadoch kubesbi silvenuch
Mishtravech suvetvi arsabach utretnavi

The geometry of the cosmos that around us lies
Is not what it seems to our eyes
It moves and changes like ice in a stream
It is fluid in nature – static form is a dream

Fluidity is the nature of life
Inflexibility invites a life of strife
The reason most resist changes that flow
Is that it is the only security they know

Divine sovereignty with the Mother is the key
It anchors us firmly thus fluid we can be
Letting graceful unfolding of life occur
No resisting change, as we are firmly anchored to Her

All of the cosmos around Her flows
We will be pulled into linear time if we let go
But in divine sovereignty our anchor is She
When She's our primary relationship, in eternal time we will be

When you feel the busy flow of life
Pull you out of your center and into strife
Stop to reconnect with the Mother
Say the words we give and envision the glory of Her

Feel the love and trust for Her
Step off life's treadmill; hold the hand of the Mother

Window 7:
To Get Information from the Dove Libraries

Barech stabavi skrunatvi
Hurset palech minestu
Rakva virskret barechvi
Utretba minevir klahurva
Skraunot slavech misutretvi vra-unas

Only when time and space have folded at last
When there is no future and there is no past
Will a portal form in a sacred space
Discovered by gods in a holy place

To the Halls of the Dove this portal leads
To call forth any information that they need
No longer to travel through tunnels themselves
To retrieve knowledge, as through stone tablets they delve

The information will come as these words they call
Announce the subject then call it forth
Those of the Order can travel there at will
But all of pure heart may use this spell

Long have they waited their magic to wield
Yet greater by far are their cosmic deeds
That which was without shall now be within
A dawning of hope and an era of grace then begins

Window 8:
To Reverse Signs of Aging

Arsaruch pribasar
Lisaret minkunash
Prichvar perusvi
Skribar elesvi

To bring back youth to face and form
To hasten the return to the youth of before
Say these words while you keep in your mind
The image of the way you looked back in time

See once again your skin fresh and firm
See how you will look when youth returns
Three times this incantation you will say
But for three months repeat every day

Window 9.
To Heal Wounds

Savet kersana misenet
Hurahastavet ekret minavesvi
Brivabet esekle brisbrahut arasta
Kars ures brihasbi ersaklut

Soothe now the memory of where pain occurred
Heal an injury with these sacred words
The body is in shock when it's been hurt
The injury's memory is cleared with these words

See in your mind the wound as though healed
Speak to the wound that the blood may congeal
Move your hand above your skin
Stroke it with love that the healing begins

Window 10:
To Create Harmony

Ukres serevet manuch beseklut
Harsapa perseprut arskrat menevit
Elsuch manavir virsetrir ares
Pruhat melseba usach mineshvravut

A doll or a photo or a painted face
Of each of antagonists on the table you place
As these words are spoken a figure eight you trace
Loop with your finger around each face

Say then these words and harmony evoke
Harmony will come from the words you spoke
Two who could not harmoniously dwell
Shall with friendship now get on well

Window 11:
To Ease Childbirth

Sprirach mersprabut
Krihet arspa speranuch
Vileset meshanut eskrumavet

Speak to the babe while yet in the womb
Soothe his fears when birth is soon
Speak these words, seven times repeat
Speak into the womb to the baby beneath

As through the birth canal the baby moves
Yet again with the incantation the newborn soothe
When baby is calm the birth is improved
It will hasten the labor and birth will come soon

Window 12:
To Evoke Twenty-four Lords of Light

Prevaklar sparetvi minusech
Privar arekba satrevi huruhat

Come with assistance a task to fulfill
Come and assist me, my Lords if you will
I call you by names most luminous and true
Help with the task I assign to you

Bishavet	*Karprahus*
Sersatu	*Sarchsavut*
Krubasat	*Istrach-klave*
Akraver	*Sutrihalastat*
Misukler	*Mekbararuch*
Nensurat	*Sihilestra*
Virabrach	*Vribelestu*
Brisbaher	*Arek-suvechvi*
Heresat	*Uplech-mistererut*
Kisanar	*Karesta*
Stuhavich	*Ustelvavi*
Esevet-brachspi	*Meneruch*

Great Lords of Light with these words call to you
If it benefits life, your request they will do

Window 13:
To Keep Childhood's Second Sight

Kaarech baravich mana sutrave
Verestatvi paranesh uska klanut harusachvi
Besetre minuvich aranesvi

At the base of the spine ninety-six cells do lie in you
Not like other cells, they never renew
The blueprint within them is held for that life
The blueprint to the pineal is conveyed up the spine

By young adulthood it is the norm
For blockages in the spine to form
As an interpretation device the pineal is the tool
For it to interpret second sight the cells provide the fuel

Without enough power second sight is lost
Being locked into the five senses becomes the cost
Daily say these words, thirty days at least
For blockages in the spine all to release

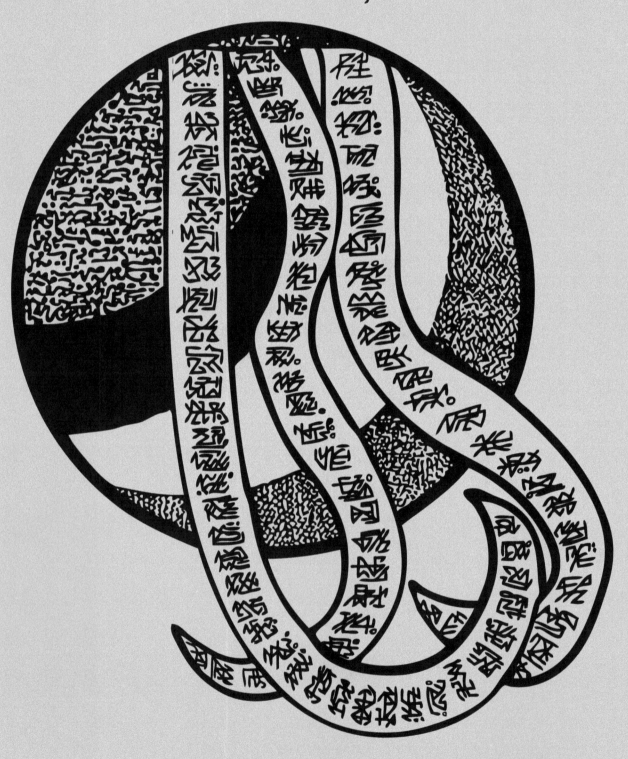

Window 14:
To Seal an Energy Drain

Marchspahut trebahech
Sukravet erastu
Sibahit nenesachvi
Kusavit ersarat

Create around you by these words you speak
Sixty-five shields to stop all energy leaks
Sixty-five times this incantation repeat
Each time you say it, you form a new shield

The shields are, you will find, a grayish blue
In between dense fields of a golden hue
State now clearly that all your intentions can pass through
The pure emotions of others can also pass through to you

The Wheel of
the Rhino's Gatee

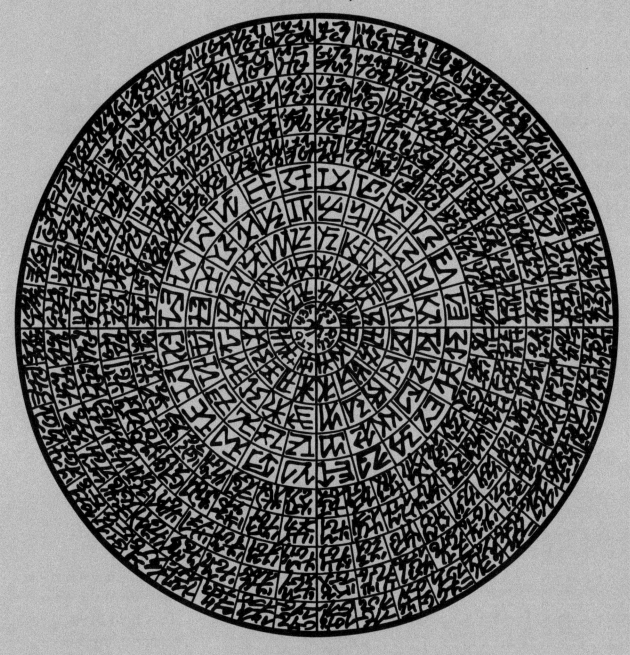

For the balance and full expression of the feminine creational codes at the base of the spine.

The codes travel up the spinal column, pushed up by rising Kundalini. They reach the pineal gland through the etheric channel. The pineal turns them into a 'universal' language carried by awareness particles.

Brain stem

The spinal fluid is filled with codes of magic, awakened when passion causes a surge of energy up the spinal column.

The pranic tube runs in a straight energy channel from the base of the spine to the top of the head (the circumference is the same as placing your middle finger and thumb together).

The original 96 cells at the base of the spine. They hold the blueprint for the individual's life.

Corpus Callosum

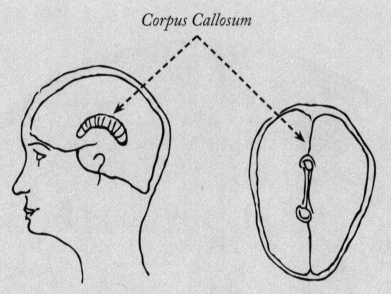

The magical codes of the left and right brain hemispheres are activated and turned by the corpus callosum into a binary code, carried by awareness particles to the pineal gland.

Pineal Gland

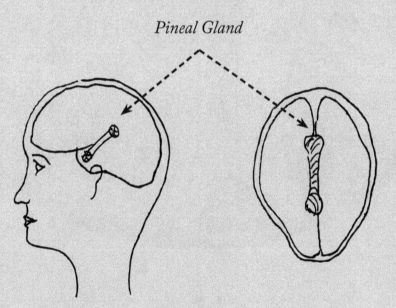

The pineal gland turns all three sets of codes into a 'universal' language and carries it to the pituitary to be directed to the specific light fibers within the 7th body of man.

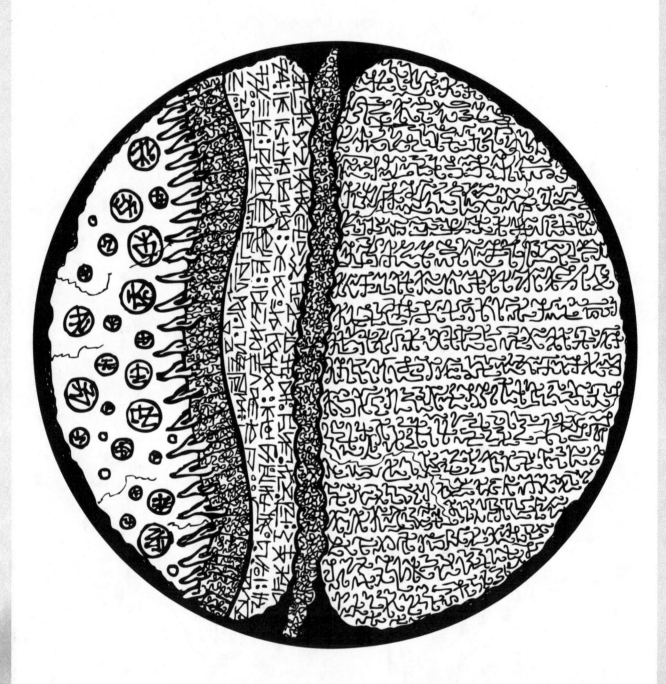

*Three sets of magical codes combine in the pituitary gland
to be directed at specific light fibers within the 7th body of man.*

Window 15:
Incorruptible Magic — Stage One

Ikrat manuvit herespi aras
Stuvit erksa neshpavi urus
Kresenach sitruvi parunes
Sikravu beres arastu

Ninety-six cells at the base of the spine
Have codes of magic that in slumber recline
Passion awakens the sleeping codes
Passion and the incantation will awaken them both

Ardently feel the desire arise
While keeping the outcome before your eyes
"Open the portal! Open it wide!
Let the fiery serpent up the spinal column rise!"

With a passionate surge, the codes awake
Feel it rise up the spine like a flame
Then the completion of the first step will be made

Window 16:
Incorruptible Magic — Stage Two

Nekva birisat herspahur urasvi
Krivanet pirabach huspavet erenus
Krihaspavet mivet eres arsatu

Codes there are that come from the spine's base
But Mother in the spinal column codes will place
Like a language of fire, awaken they will
As the pranic tube the spine with sacred fire fills

The incantation will call forth the spinal codes
As the codes from the spine's base rise from their abode
Interacting with the spinal codes as upward they rise
Serpent magic now will fully arise

Up through the heart and into the brain it goes
Carried by the pranic tube the magic will rise
Into the pineal rise these codes
To this interpretive center the magic codes go

Window 17:
Incorruptible Magic — Stage Three

Nensarak stubavech sechvanut
Usut misanach erestrahur
Karsanat harstu mivech pahur

The Mother in wisdom in the right-brain created
Codes of magic that must now be awakened
Use these words to activate the codes
Frequency-based are the codes of the Rose

The codes thus awakened must be loved into being
Acknowledge with love the desired outcomes seen
Is there aught wrong–then forgiveness you give
Acknowledging that external events are created within

Co-created have you whatever must be changed
Now in love it must be destructured, as within you changes are made
Envelop with understanding, but with fervent desires
That life to a higher order aspires

Window 18:
Incorruptible Magic — Stage Four

Kavahut eset misenech harastu
Esbech ruvetvi misdanavoch heravi
Bliset eskra vivetvi minavit eras

"Awaken, oh codes that in the left-brain lie!
Awaken encodings of the language of light
By these words I invoke you, come to life!
By the power of this incantation, I command you arise!"

By the power of your intent so it shall be
The codes here slumbering awakened shall be
Then magical codes in sets of three
Awakened codes of fire, love and light shall be

The Orders of these codes magic orders are
They shall work together from different lands from far
So too within you cooperation should be
Between these centers in the body holding codes in sets of three

Window 19:
Incorruptible Magic — Stage Five

Haranot keret aratu sabahit
Kisanit etret brivat vibrasvi
Kluharavit esetvavi minatretvi

Take now the codes of the left and the right
Into the callosum pull them with love and light
Say these words by the Mother bestowed
The incantation that to the callosum calls the codes

The callosum a doorway for awareness becomes
The left-brain's and the right's codes there become one
The callosum's awareness holds binary codes
The left and the right-brain's codes cling to those

Thus a common language for these two sets are found
In the awareness that in the callosum abounds
The language of light and love now are one
As information-laden awareness particles form

Window 20:
Incorruptible Magic — Stage Six

Nenseratut haraset ublat blavi
Mensevech piharaset stretvavi
Kersavit brihet arsakla prihes
Bruvesbavi mineset etret uvaranas

Now this information from the callosum must be called
By the words of magic call it forth
The greatest interpretive terminal within man
Is that portal of awareness, the pineal gland

The awareness that holds the binary codes
Now from the callosum to the pineal flows
To join there the codes that from the spinal column come
That in the pineal three languages become one

The Wheel of the
Lion's Gate

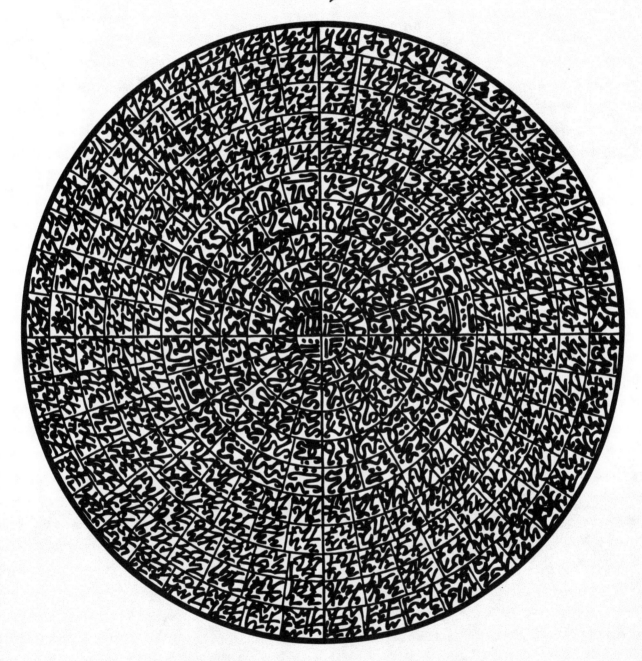

*To bring balance to the masculine energies, silencing the clamor of the
mind and allowing for better interpretation of subtle information by the pineal gland.*

Window 21:
Incorruptible Magic — Stage Seven

Karesba esatru bisenet harusat
Velenes struhes arasatva hereset
Sutvabit esekle mihasvravit
Kranus esutvatvi misetret haru anas

The pineal a gateway for information that flows
It can create a common language for all three sets of codes
For it receives awareness from the Mother's heart
Awareness particles constructed from three different parts

The tertiary codes to this awareness will cling
The law of polarity this attraction brings
But an interfacing language it will provide
For the codes of fire, love and light

Say the words of magic that allow the awareness to flow
The words of magic will form the tertiary codes
A universal language of the three sets of codes
Will have been born so that magic will flow

Window 22:
Incorruptible Magic — Stage Eight

Kesh harvavit esechvi usutras
Nenhar sabahut ekleverevat
Nensahach skerevat sklerutpraha
Misanach viresat harastu urekbi

A tube has been formed from the pineal to the third eye
To the pituitary, the seat of second sight
The pituitary has turned, by Mother decreed
To metamorphose man, for this there was a need

Facing inwards now not out anymore
The third eye looks inward not out as before
The etheric tube, by the Mother Goddess made
For the restoration of white magic man will aid

Call by the incantation's words
Call the awareness through the tube by words that are pure
Let awareness carry the magic's codes
Let three sets of magic's codes to the third eye flow

Window 23:
Incorruptible Magic — Stage Nine

Mishet unach haras eskle heresat brivabet
Ninhurek prihebas skrevanut sabata
Misenech vilshperet merenach husbavi

Now great magic by the pituitary is done
The materialization of magic now has begun
The pituitary fueled by passion's dictates
Directs its focus to the inner landscape

By finding within what in exterior mirrors may be
That which created the external similarly
Do you wish more abundantly to live
What areas of life do you withhold love you can give

Travelling along the lines of focus within
The flow of magic carried by awareness begins
The particles carrying the awareness's codes
To the corresponding fibers of light[14] will go

Now the heart must love and forgiveness emanate
Towards that which is within, for the outside to change
Say the words while the focus is held
While the heart extends love as well

14. The light fibers in the 7th body of man.

Window 24:
Incorruptible Magic — Stage Ten

Krihat kluvater nenseruk brihespi
Biharanas kri-esena sahut privesbi
Karatu sihuravi pihuranat
Krives varatu misenet

The seventh body of man of many light fibers consists
The light fibers within mirror realities that externally exist
Lights up light fibers within, it affects their external counterparts

When inner light fibers are activated and changed
Within exterior light fibers changes are also made
The words you say will hasten effects
The changes without that the inner reflects

The light fibers within by magic lit
Will in turn change the exterior with it
When light fibers within the bodies of one
Light external fibers, a first cause he has become

Angels Called for Stage Ten

Karuchba	Misbaravech
Misbahurunat	Akranenasvi
Misenetvrahur	Huklet-arat
Kli-usaravet	Vruhesarachvi
Persperena	Nensurarava

The Shield to Safeguard the Magic of the Lords of Light

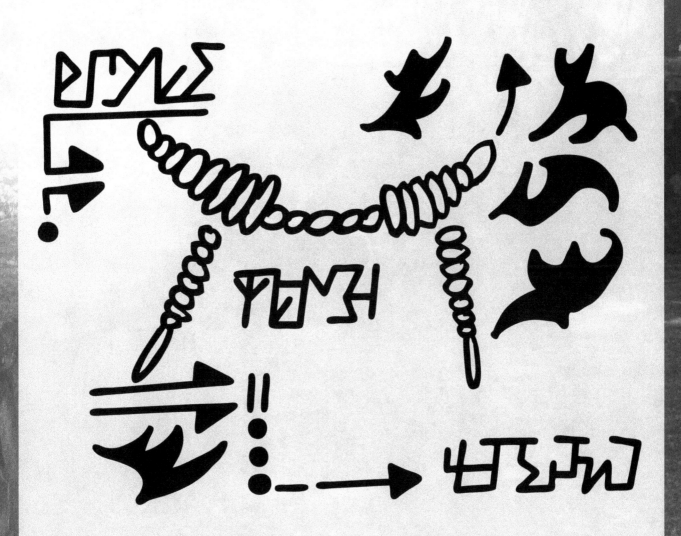

Ashanach bruhach mestet uskaranut braha

254

Preparations for the Magical Life from the Dragon Kingdom

The Sacred Fires
of the Hadji-ka

Preparation for the Magical Life

The information given by the custodians of these sacred records, the dragons of Avondar, is life-altering in its scope and power. The magical life is as natural to them as breathing, requiring no learnt methodology.

The powerful influence of these sacred records, is designed to restore the magic of man in two ways: firstly by removing the blockages to these innate and natural abilities, and secondly, to enhance consciousness through increased perception. With increased consciousness comes increased resources and hence, also enhanced abilities.

The crux of the magical life is the reduction of the gap between cause and effect; between intent and manifestation. To achieve this, density has to be decreased. The removal of illusions can be called the main purpose of this book. It is also the key to magic by reducing density in our lives.

May these holy records and their groundbreaking revelations restore the precious heritage of man; A life of incorruptible white magic.

Dragon over Glastonbury

Dragon Affirmations
for the Spine and Brain Stem

1. I am beginningless and endless. (C1)
2. I am shadowless. (C2)
3. I release all personality. (C3)
4. I awaken to the fullness of my being. (C4)
5. I am surrendered to Infinite Intent. (C5)
6. The currents of eternity flow through me. (C6)
7. I am the one and the many. (C7)
8. I am open to receive from myself. (T1)
9. I am fulfilled beyond my expectations. (T2)
10. I fluidly anticipate abundant existence. (T3)
11. I respond to the Intent of the Eternal Being. (T4)
12. I see the ever-newness of eternity. (T5)
13. I am in complete Oneness through Surrender. (T6)
14. I release all need to control outcome. (T7)
15. I exist authentically. (T8)
16. I am an unfolding work of art. (T9)
17. I dwell in the eternal peace of integrated co-operation. (T10)
18. I simultaneously observe and participate. (T11)
19. I rest in the labor of being. (T12)
20. I am the poetic perspective. (L1)
21. I delight in the beauty of my being. (L2)
22. I find my eternal presence in all. (L3)
23. I move through all expressions of existence. (L4)
24. I experience fusion through resonance. (L5)

Working with the
Dragon Affirmations

Repeat the affirmation and internalize them. Do this right at the time of sleeping and of awakening as you are working at the bridge between the realms of soul (the dreamtime) and body (the awake time).

Spiritual people have long tried to clear their daily lives from illusions, however fail to recognize that the dreamtime too, is their responsibility. The dreamtime or soul worlds are just as real as the physical reality, in that they both are part of the larger Dream that we call duality. However, we take responsibility for one (the physical) but not for the other (the dreamtime). Thus all the hard self-examination one does in the daytime can be undone by perceptions and actions in the dreamtime.

The Affirmations of the Spine carry the perception and purity of vision of one's whole being through from the physical to the dreamtime. There they clear debris and old belief systems that are held within physicality in the spinal cord. With it responsibility is taken for one's whole reality, both the awake time and the dreamtime.

Repeat these affirmations for 30-60 days, depending on how much programming you have or still hold on to.

Healing and Balancing the Spine

The magic held in the spine can also be accessed according to the time of the day. Refer to the Lemurian Clock of the Depth of Living for the specific time for each vertebra. To promote healing and balancing of the spine, draw or trace the sigils for the relevant vertebra.

Sigils for the Spine and Brain Stem

The magic held in the spinal cord is also accessed according to the time of the day.

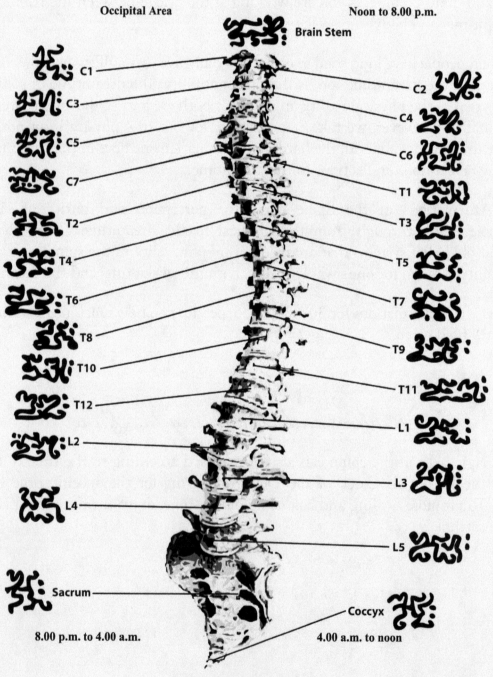

Occipital Area

Noon to 8.00 p.m.

Brain Stem

C1
C3
C5
C7
T2
T4
T6
T8
T10
T12
L2
L4
Sacrum

C2
C4
C6
T1
T3
T5
T7
T9
T11
L1
L3
L5
Coccyx

8.00 p.m. to 4.00 a.m.

4.00 a.m. to noon

Mechpa hurures arsat

260

The Lemurian
Clock of the Depth of Living

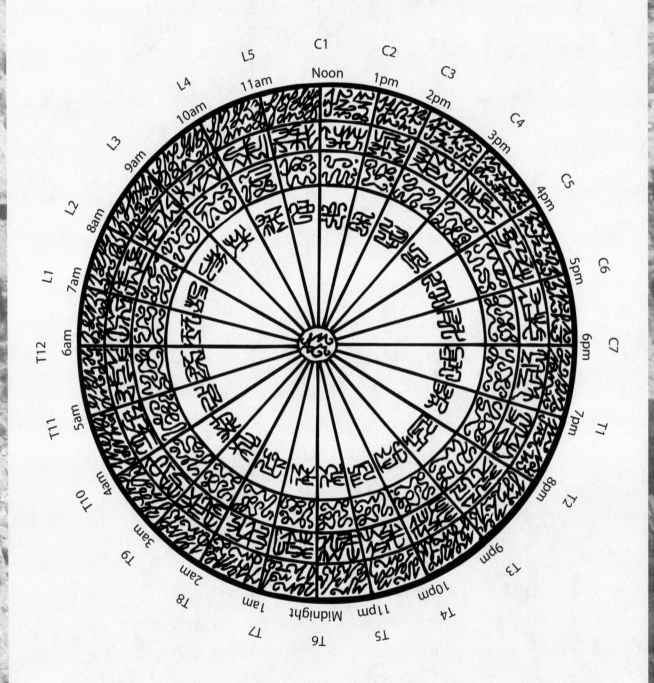

Mirek stanavi sklibaru harsta mivek arechbava hursta

The 24 Wheels of Neshba to Open the Dragon Gates of the Spine

1. Birchsparet-hevenasvi

There are periods of reason and deduction and periods of effortless knowing of inevitability. The times of reason produce form and structure. The times of non-cognitive knowing produce fluid formlessness and destructuring. Jointly, they produce eternal moments and the gaps between the moments. Timelessness is produced by living them as one – knowing the inevitable and with reasoning, finding out why it is so.

2. Blishbretbraha-avaneski

The feminine perspective does not like to be definitive and precise. The masculine on the other hand, thrives on it. The tendency to confuse and delay the conclusion of the masculine's plans and agendas has been seen by the masculine as being obstructive. The masculine's tendency to demand a controlled outcome has been seen by the feminine as controlling and dictatorial. In cooperative integration it must be appreciated that the feminine's lack of preciseness leaves gateways of higher possibilities open. It provides openings for alchemical leveraging into higher and unforeseen outcomes. The masculine conclusiveness allows this fluid potential to actualize into manifestation.

3. Michba-erenechspavi

Impurity is the stage of creation of form; the process of clustering the resources of existence into shapes. That which is interpreted as purity, is the release of the inner tension that maintains form. Impurity blocks the flow of unfolding existence and dams up resources to produce form. Impurity, from the heart's standpoint, is the linear movement of mind. From the mind's standpoint, it is the circular movement of emotion in a seemingly chaotic manner. As all opposites do, the one begets the other. They work together to produce fluid form – the playground of indivisible, Infinite existence.

4. Kuhu-uret-avastra

Honor is a mind-made concept that arises from the fact that the feminine has for eons suppressed itself so that the masculine could grow. Honor is the living of programmed protocols. In polarity, more of one pole is less of the other. The masculine's inner feminine and masculine has become whole and mature. The feminine has only its feminine pole functioning. This has made it unable to interpret its own experiences since the electrical, masculine component interprets the memories held by the feminine. The protection of honor is the masculine making sure that it protectively surrounds the feminine so that all experiences can be interpreted. It surrounds it by producing matrices that have to be continually produced as the feminine pushes beyond them—hence the search of the masculine to understand.

5. Skuhu-ustrech-velesvi

The judgment of the masculine, seeing itself as responsible for the feminine which it sees as irresponsible, is because it does not see the larger perfection of how they work together. The masculine desires to contain, which the feminine interprets as control. The feminine desires to be free of boundaries, which the masculine interprets as irresponsible since she cannot interpret her experience when she leaves the boundaries of his interpretation. The way these opposing desires work together is that, the masculine (perception) keeps having to expand to match the expansion of the feminine (emotion) and in this way, the self is systematically explored; the unknown turned into the known through experience.

6. Spere-hespa-klubanet

The awake state (life's realm) has become more real than the dream state (death's realm) because it got stuck. This happened because the feminine, not understanding the value of its uninterpreted emotion, and feeling itself to be unwhole, lost the self-confidence of expression. Authentic impulses of expression should be regarded as valid, even if the perfection of the large picture cannot be seen.

7. Kerch-spibaresvi

The masculine is afraid of what it cannot control. The feminine is afraid of being controlled. It is this opposing agenda that creates the tension that sustains the cohesive form of the cosmos. The masculine provides form and the feminine provides growth. This creates the harmonious interplay of structure and flow.

8. Nichsta-erek-hursavi

The masculine has lived the masculine pole and the feminine pole. The feminine became balanced when the Atlantean information of the 300 angels was released. Atlantis represented the masculine pole of the Earth – North America now represents it. The neutral pole (Western Europe +/– and Eastern Europe –/+), will be expressed by both when the 75 dragon windows yield their insights.

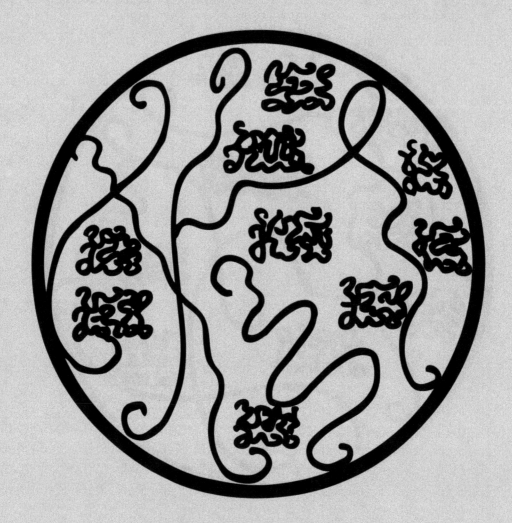

9. Mishba-ukret-ninusklat

Of the 75 insights, 25 are of the awake world (the masculine perception based reality) and 50 are of the soul realms or dream world, and are non-cognitive realizations of the perfect harmonious interplay of the seeming opposition of the masculine and feminine. These insights jointly will allow the masculine and feminine to express its neutral. Their interplay will be seen as a romantic dance exploring the poetry of existence, rather than a war.

10. Klet-versparut-unachvi

Lemuria was the Motherland. Now Russia fulfills this role, representing the feminine on Earth. The feminine's masculine will be brought into balance by the release of a set of Lemurian records that contain the knowledge of the 300 Lemurian angels of black light and frequency. The balancing of the feminine's 3 poles prepares the body for its second stage of resurrection.

11. Sitru-beleverechbi-sparut

When the feminine is balanced, the pranic tube is prepared to enter the spinal cord. Its frequency becomes elevated to balance the light that is found in the spinal cord of one who is balanced in his or her masculine, so that a marriage between equals can take place. Three layers of sheaths surround the spinal cord, each one holding memories and representing jointly the masculine matrix of physical life. The matrices of existence also consist of 3 layers (masculine, feminine and neutral).

12. Su-uhanesvi-krihastat

A resurrected being has 300 strands of DNA that become activated during the 2nd stage, when the pranic tube (which contains 300 sound or frequency chambers of DNA in the form of a large rose) merges with the spinal cord. The spinal cord is comprised of 300 strands (electrical) that merge with the 300 magnetic frequency chambers of the pranic tube in a marriage of light and frequency.

13. Michpa-uhavanesbi-arat

The first stage of resurrection enables one to take charge of one's soul reality as experienced in the dream time. This allows you to maintain your integrity and high level of self-responsibility in the dream reality as much as in the awake reality. They are both equally real and have the same value. The second stage allows you to move into the sleep state while awake and into an awakened state while asleep. Death and rebirth have no hold on you.

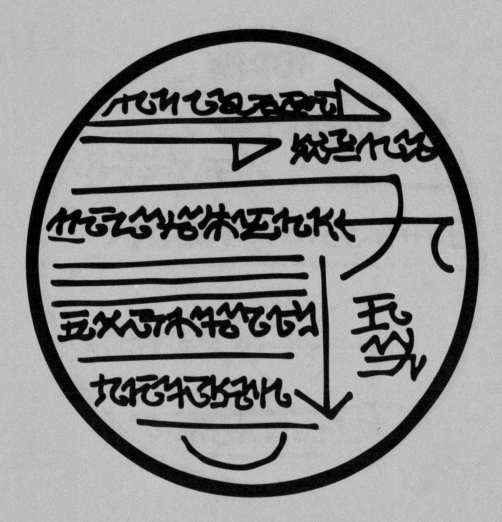

14. Plihastre-uhavabat

There is a third stage of resurrection, called the magic life, in which the dream state and awakened state merge and become one. Because it is only in the physical where the delay between cause and effect is as much as it is (the denser life is, the greater the delay), this merging that makes life less dense, produces the magic of more immediate manifestation (the definition of white magic).

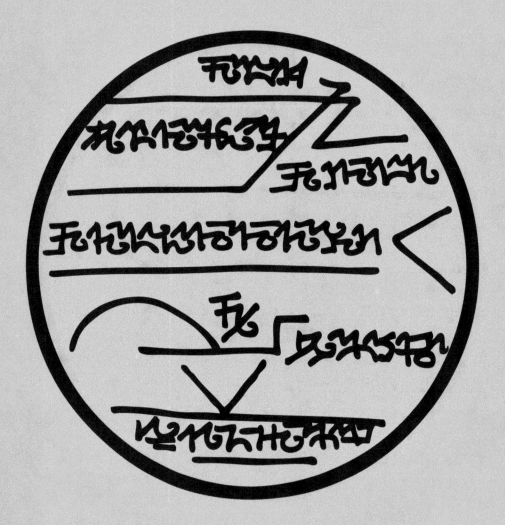

15. Mechpa-spi-uraket

The feminine is regarded as pure, and mistakenly attributed with qualities that pertain only to the higher realms, and that it need not concern itself with the details of everyday life. But in the harmonious interplay of masculine and feminine, the masculine holds a known space for the feminine to explore the depth of the unknown. The unknown reveals itself through the experiences of everyday life.

16. Blihavarespi-skrahuraset

Not only does the masculine provide the horizons that surround the unknown, which the feminine wishes to explore (the surrounding matrix), but also the reference point from which to observe this exploration; the little self. This observation point observes and analyzes the feminine exploration of the unknown and turns it into the known through analysis. It then files it in its library – the matrix. When the feminine moves beyond its horizon of observation, it expands to incorporate it.

17. Meshba-ste-ehelechvi

The origin of masculine and feminine come from the Infinite's attention and intention. The origin of the masculine is attention and the origin of the feminine is intention. The attention of the Infinite is that which defines the space in which creation will take place. Space is masculine. The intention that creates the details, is the movement that fills in the space. This is like a foundation that is dug so that a house can be built within its parameters. The bricks, windows and doors are the details. The flow of creating the details is time, which is feminine.

18. Bribash-merenechvi

The plan of the whole house is the one, and the filling in of the details represents the many. The masculine has become representative of the many and the feminine, as the one. This is the opposite of the true nature of each. This indicates that we are dealing with mirrors, since mirrors always reflect the opposite of what is.

19. Archvanet-plivabechspi

The question "Who am I?" only arose within the Infinite when artistic expression took place. This created the first relationship: "Who am I in relationship to my expression?" The search for the answer created the second relationship, beyond the one who expresses and the expression. The second relationship became the observer and the observed. This created opposites and changed the expression of the Infinite to a new purpose: A reflection of the Infinite.

20. Neserek-priharastat

In order for anything to be studied, the concept of what is and what is not has to exist. As the Infinite studied Itself in the mirror, the concept that there are things in existence that the Infinite is not was born. This reduced Its self-image from "I am everything" to "I am some things". This gave rise to the concept of boundaries and the protection of them to avoid being invaded by what is not.

21. Ekre-viharsparut

This concept of anything outside of Itself existing, reduced the Infinite's vastness by introducing self-reflection: the attempt to define the undefinable. The miniscule reflection as an 'opposite' of Itself, further diminished Its self-conception. The possibility that there could be knowledge lacking about what It is not, created the concept that It had to 'acquire' it. This created the illusion of linear becoming, or growth and evolution.

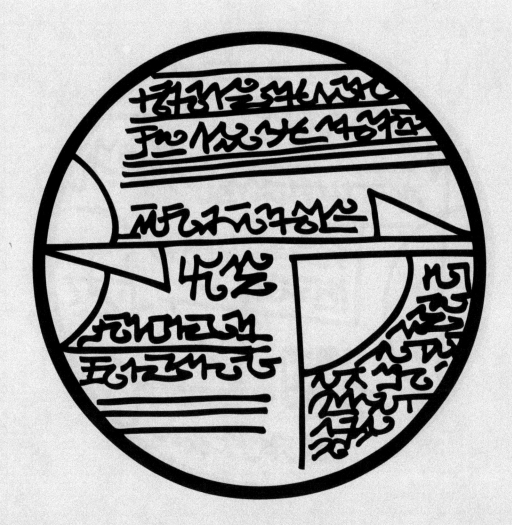

22. Eleklet-visel-uhavastra

To study Its expression, the Infinite analyzed it. This pulled the expression apart so that Its pieces could be observed. The shadow that fell formed an electromagnetic substance; the building blocks of life and death – the substance of shadow. During death, the frequency component of these subatomic particles is more dominant. During life, light is more prevalent.

23. Pirit-akre-vivas-haranesvi

What is paid attention to through examination lingers and stays, giving the appearance of permanence. The longevity of a manifestation depends on whether we think it is there. When examining something, we are not living or expressing something else. Where there is no expression of parts of ourselves, addiction sets in. The Infinite created an Embodiment for Itself by making Itself the expresser and not the expressed. In examining Its expression, it kept it in place. The Infinite's Embodiment then wanted to 'save' Its expression for It had become addicted to having it there. The concept of an expression, which became a mirror, now became a Creation.

24. Kretna-stihubalesvi

When we try and save what is in the mirror of our environment, it will do the opposite back, as all mirrors do. The Infinite, having engaged Its own expression for so long, had no memory of what had gone before. Memory does not exist where experience does not, and experience requires self-reflection. Self-reflection began when the Infinite studied Itself in Its expression. Remembering no other existence, It kept Its 'Creation' in place by entering into it and fixing it. Mirrors are opposite also in their response to our actions. The Embodiment had tried to build up and strengthen Its creation, while the Cosmos tried to reduce and undermine the Embodiment of the Infinite amidst itself.

The Shield to Safeguard the Magic of the Dragons

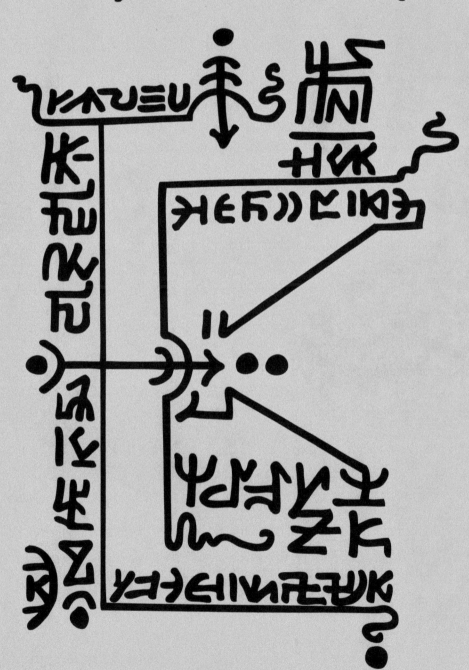

Magic through Emphasis

The Magic of the Gods in Conjunction with the Angel Gods

Photo taken by Raj in his garden.

Magic for Perpetual Self-Regeneration

Third Ring Magic of the Gods

First ring magic uses external sources and allies to effect changes in reality. Second ring magic changes the world by changing within. Third ring magic uses integrated cooperation between inner realities and external allies to create outer circumstances through inner emphases.

The DNA strand of a god-being has 300 strands, or frequency chambers, in the first and second levels of godhood, and 441 DNA strands in the third level of godhood. This represents the 441 frequency components of the cosmos. Cosmic events can be orchestrated by emphasizing certain corresponding chambers within the DNA. This is the basis for third ring magic: *Magic Through Emphasis — The Magic of the Gods.*

The external allies that are used are the 441 angel gods that preside over the cosmic frequency chambers. Their assignments are encoded in letter and number combinations, and different templates are used for different purposes. A specific DNA chamber (or 'petal') may have one letter / number combination for the magic of self-regeneration of the cells, and another for the magic of successful business.

Each magical purpose has a specific number of principles. Each principle has a sigil, and five angel gods that respond to that sigil.

Each principle's five angels (each with its own code) are involved in drawing that principle's sigil. This is done until all sigils for all principles (30, in the case of the magic for the regeneration of the cells) are complete.

How to Prepare for the Magical Ceremony

Study the Principles of Self-regeneration prior to doing the ceremony. Take time to consider the benefits that may result from living these principles.

To draw the sigils yourself, you will need 30 copies of the numbered rose template (1 for each sigil). Alternatively, the pre-drawn sigils may be used, in which case you will trace over all thirty of them with your finger prior to doing the ceremony.

Each sigil has a number (for ease of identifying the correct petal when drawing the sigil and is not used in the ceremony), an angel name and a code. The example below is for the first principle for cellular regeneration.

16	Erseta –	**ST11**
84	Ururuk –	**49ST**
124	Hesetu –	**69L**
8	Prihanit –	**FBDX**
438	Eseklet-nisar –	**TLPC**

Drawing the Sigils

The sigil is drawn on a numbered rose template. When creating the first sigil, start by drawing a little circle on petal 16 of the numbered template. Draw a straight line from there to petal 84, then to 124, and on to 8. From 8, draw a straight line to 438, and from there to the center of the rose, where the line ends at the inner circle.

Place the sigil's template face down on the table next to you and continue creating the next sigil until you have drawn all 30. As you complete each sigil, place it upside down on top of the previous one. You are creating a stack of 30 sigils, with the first one on top and the 30th one at the bottom when you turn the stack over.

Using the pre-drawn sigils

If you are using the pre-drawn sigils, it is important that you trace each of the sigils one-by-one with your finger. This is done prior to creating the stack that goes below your feet.

Say the following incantation:

Trehach menuset arasta

Follow the instructions on the next page to create the stack of images for below your feet.

Note: For ease of printing, the sacred tools for this ceremony are available as a free download. Scan the QR code or visit

WWW.IAMPRESENCE.COM/SPELLS/GODS

How to do the Ceremony

For this ceremony you will be lying down either on the floor, your bed or a massage table. There are two stacks of sacred images: one will be placed under you mid-back, below the navel area, and the other is below your feet.

Stack 1:

Make a stack of the *30 Sigils of the Principles of Perpetual Self-regeneration.*
Number 1 will be at the top, number 30 on the bottom.
Place the *Rose Template of Codes* <u>below</u> the 30 sigils.
Place the *DNA Rose* <u>below</u> the rose template of codes.
Align the dots and clip the stack together to prevent displacement.
Place the stack below your feet as you lie down on your back.

Stack 2:

Place the stack of the 441 angel names beneath your back (behind the navel).

Performing the Ceremony:

1. Have the list of the *30 Principles of Perpetual Self-regeneration* with their codes and angels in your hand.
2. Focusing on one principle at a time, read the names of the 5 angels and the codes, and as you do, feel the relevant sigil move all the way up along your body, in through your feet and out the top of your head.
3. When you have envisioned all 30 sigils moving through you, then envision the *Rose Template with the Codes*, followed by the *DNA Rose*[15] move through you from your feet all the way up and out through the top of your head.
4. End by saying:

> *May the necessary DNA chambers be activated to bring about the Perpetual Self-regeneration of the incorruptible matter of my body. May the angel gods support this by activating the corresponding cosmic components.*

---

15. The DNA Rose represents a cross-section of an advanced god being's DNA, showing frequency chambers as petals. It is also representative of a cosmic template. The cosmos has the same pattern of 'sound chambers' as the DNA strand.

The Principles and Codes of Self-regeneration

01 *Self-sustaining emotional self-sovereignty*

16	Erseta	**ST11**
84	Ururuk	**49ST**
124	Hesetu	**69L**
8	Prihanit	**FBDX**
438	Eseklet-nisar	**TLPC**

02 *Self-contained energy production*

98	Setplanis	**LSTP**
14	Setlvra	**LBD**
402	Helsata	**0QZ**
319	Ritva-balanuk	**396**
22	Litklevu	**R32**

03 *Fully-used, complete pranic circuit*

3	Kasava	**SP1KL**
21	Irksaba	**9PQ**
107	Kersanu	**MN8**
68	Sterabit	**XPL2**
409	Rutvrabi	**11-2B**

04 *Masterful directiveness within complete surrender*

13	Elishur	**R2S**
106	Suhitar	**HIK**
92	Araksut	**186PT**
306	Sunuvish-baver	**KP2**
83	Menetra	**32K**

05 *Withdrawing from the games of mirrors*

168	Erektu	**V3P**
32	Esteva	**TL4**
418	Kirivirspata	**11-18**
61	Iranut	**92-LP**
16	Erseta	**ST11**

06 *Existence beyond body, soul and spirit*

298	Harasatvi-balush	**926**
86	Bitrenek	**FRTV**
113	Narekva	**2P9L**
28	Kusana	**SL6**
440	Nukbara	**VKL**

07 *Timelessness through surrender*

99	Risita	**RWXP**
111	Brihanu	**32LV**
34	Ikbarut	**3BQ**
6	Ritsahur	**KPL2**
108	Mektaru	**L2T**

08 *Fluid release of linear time*

44	Mileves	**04P**
308	Eleshner	**VR2**
92	Araksut	**186PT**
11	Nenesa	**S19H**
86	Bitrenek	**FRTV**

09 *Spacelessness through appreciative perspectives*

16	Erseta	**ST11**
410	Hanasat	**4TS**
116	Ninerek	**3H5L**
324	Suhach-ornit	**VSP**
19	Iresta	**SQL**

10 *Existing as the impervious source of our reality*

110	Vilestu	**MP9**
62	Subarut	**3R6**
402	Helsata	**0QZ**
317	Serchsavir	**QRS**
86	Bitrenek	**FRTV**

11 *Innovative dancer of the eternal song*

116	Ninerek	**3H5L**
264	Asabak-akrich	**KS99**
98	Setplanis	**LSTP**
211	Hurusut	**LST8**
4	Ritubi	**N26-11**

12 *Allowing the joyous shaping of our ever-renewing form*

89	Lineret	**XKUT**
164	Kavanit	**95Q**
32	Esteva	**TL4**
116	Ninerek	**3H5L**
72	Isanus	**XL28**

13 *Delightful miracle of expression as form*

160	Resavit	**SB2**
432	Nasaru	**3SX**
86	Bitrenek	**FRTV**
114	Kirsena	**XYST**
3	Kasava	**SP1KL**

14 *Inspired enthusiasm of self-regenerating form*

12	Rusana	**KS2L**
326	Biraset	**32S**
81	Setpliher	**VP9**
92	Araksut	**186PT**
6	Ritsahur	**KPL2**

15 *Victorious expression of incorruptible matter*

184	Gravanik	**14P**
28	Kusana	**SL6**
69	Rasanur	**46BD**
421	Herenit	**KPS**
18	Pruhanas	**MO6**

16 *Strengthened conviction of miraculous existence*

62	Subarut	**3R6**
31	Lukvanot	**R2S**
16	Erseta	**ST11**
214	Rutpahur	**6T-S11**
408	Hesta-misech	**HZV**

17 *Marveling at the awakened gifts of the body*

119	Retsavi	**19ST**
23	Ristave	**KS2**
84	Ururuk	**49ST**
316	Meshpahur-akrat	**PA2**
298	Harasatvi-balush	**926**

18 *Interpretive dancer of the joyous dance of Infinite expression*

80	Rinahur	**L2T3**
61	Iranut	**92-LP**
312	Gelshanadoch	**LPT**
98	Setplanis	**LSTP**
16	Erseta	**ST11**

19 *The gentle guidance of the subtle currents of the ocean of Infinite existence*

140	Arakva	**2BD**
116	Ninerek	**3H5L**
380	Nereksu	**VRX**
6	Ritsahur	**KPL2**
91	Arsata	**HRK4**

20 *Childlike wonderment and glad expectations*

14	Setlvra	**LBD**
83	Menetra	**32K**
46	Setkranat	**94PT**
418	Kirivirspata	**11-18**
321	Prekpranuhish	**ST3**

21 *Open receptivity to the unfathomable wonders of existence*

110	Vilestu	**MP9**
210	Nenklitparu	**32SF**
93	Pisiter	**LT45**
2	Mistaba	**NX4-6**
11	Nenesa	**S19H**

22 *The adventure of never-ending, aware self-discovery*

16	Erseta	**ST11**
46	Setkranat	**94PT**
391	Kiranat	**LPHV**
429	Barastu	**R20**
112	Silvatu	**KRS**

23 *Freedom from limiting expectations by readiness to be amazed*

16	Erseta	**ST11**
92	Araksut	**186PT**
247	Harsat-manuvech	**41ST**
122	Asavit	**KV13**
84	Ururuk	**49ST**

24 *Self-generated inspiration for the graceful artistry of expression*

62	Subarut	**3R6**
81	Setpliher	**VP9**
329	Sutrivat	**PL2**
168	Erektu	**V3P**
26	Skarut	**2SK**

25 *Cooperation of individuality within inclusiveness*

81	Setpliher	**VP9**
416	Ukreta	**SK16**
291	Platplasur	**XPL2**
362	Karatu	**LV5**
17	Niretu	**04T**

26 *Living with deliberate reverence through awareness*

114	Kirsena	**XYST**
83	Menetra	**32K**
42	Harchtu	**P3L**
61	Iranut	**92-LP**
320	Niskaret	**QP11**

27 *Archetypal awareness of the potency of choices*

16	Erseta	**ST11**
43	Setar	**9WK**
389	Ranuret	**SL16**
118	Esetur	**LK14**
26	Skarut	**2SK**

28 *Effortless movement through eternity*

84	Ururuk	**49ST**
42	Harchtu	**P3L**
169	Melkor	**LBX**
32	Esteva	**TL4**
319	Ritva-balanuk	**396**

29 *Being our own source of boundless vitality*

169	Melkor	**LBX**
32	Esteva	**TL4**
419	Nensarahik	**VSRT**
22	Litklevu	**R32**
318	Kirsh-pater	**L8P**

30 *Effortless miraculous achievements without end*

72	Isanus	**XL28**
183	Nanasit	**SL9**
416	Ukreta	**SK16**
86	Bitrenek	**FRTV**
391	Kiranat	**LPHV**

The Awakening of the
30 Principles of Perpetual Self-regeneration

1. Self-sustaining emotional self-sovereignty
2. Self-contained energy production
3. Fully-used, complete pranic circuit
4. Masterful directiveness within complete surrender
5. Withdrawing from the games of mirrors
6. Existence beyond body, soul and spirit
7. Timelessness through surrender
8. Fluid release of linear time
9. Spacelessness through appreciative perspectives
10. Existing as the impervious source of our reality
11. Innovative dancer of the eternal song
12. Allowing the joyous shaping of our ever-renewing form
13. Delightful miracle of expression as form
14. Inspired enthusiasm of self-regenerating form
15. Victorious expression of incorruptible matter
16. Strengthened conviction of miraculous existence
17. Marveling at the awakened gifts of the body
18. Interpretive dancer of the joyous dance of Infinite expression
19. The gentle guidance of the subtle currents of the ocean of Infinite existence
20. Childlike wonderment and glad expectations
21. Open receptivity to the unfathomable wonders of existence
22. The adventure of never-ending, aware self-discovery
23. Freedom from limiting expectations by readiness to be amazed
24. Self-generated inspiration for the graceful artistry of expression
25. Cooperation of individuality within inclusiveness
26. Living with deliberate reverence through awareness
27. Archetypal awareness of the potency of choices
28. Effortless movement through eternity
29. Being our own source of boundless vitality
30. Effortless miraculous achievements without end

The 441 Angel Gods

1. Saavech
2. Mistaba
3. Kasava
4. Ritubi
5. Klisva
6. Ritsahur
7. Elsena
8. Prihanit
9. Kirtlva
10. Rekpa
11. Nenesa
12. Rusana
13. Elishur
14. Setlvra
15. Sitklavis
16. Erseta
17. Niretu
18. Pruhanas
19. Iresta
20. Kruvrabi
21. Irksaba
22. Litklevu
23. Ristave
24. Arunas
25. Elerus
26. Skarut
27. Ertreve
28. Kusana
29. Pelevri
30. Eksavi
31. Lukvanot
32. Esteva
33. Rasanut
34. Ikbarut
35. Liseter
36. Nensarat

37. Ekselva
38. Kusaru
39. Nesbasur
40. Kiranur
41. Utraver
42. Harchtu
43. Setar
44. Mileves
45. Hirklana
46. Setkranat
47. Usbranot
48. Nekbarot
49. Elsavur
50. Sitklar
51. Viresat
52. Kuraset
53. Erkplasur
54. Siterek
55. Ilsavit
56. Menevech
57. Harsurat
58. Ikbarnot
59. Krusavek
60. Tribarut
61. Iranut
62. Subarut
63. Ekparahut
64. Viseklech
65. Barvanuk
66. Lisetar
67. Muniter
68. Sterabit
69. Rasanur
70. Kripahar
71. Arasuter
72. Isanus

73. Misahur
74. Kurunis
75. Elsador
76. Nurata
77. Pirahur
78. Eskevre
79. Plehitar
80. Rinahur
81. Setpliher
82. Esklesir
83. Menetra
84. Ururuk
85. Seklevra
86. Bitrenek
87. Reksavi
88. Ekbaratuk
89. Lineret
90. Pelehur
91. Arsata
92. Araksut
93. Pisiter
94. Karsana
95. Ekranur
96. Hurutat
97. Sakravi
98. Setplanis
99. Risita
100. Arakna
101. Mechba-surat
102. Hersetu
103. Lakshmet
104. Rutvaba
105. Nechtaru
106. Suhitar
107. Kersanu
108. Mektaru

109. Retvavik
110. Vilestu
111. Brihanu
112. Silvatu
113. Narekva
114. Kirsena
115. Retsahur
116. Ninerek
117. Kilshebas
118. Esetur
119. Retsavi
120. Menenus
121. Karsharanut
122. Asavit
123. Eklet-brabit
124. Hesetu
125. Misarut
126. Arsahur
127. Mesenech
128. Elvavis
129. Kisarut
130. Helsatur
131. Mananes
132. Sihet-arasta
133. Eksuravit
134. Menet-klarit
135. Asur
136. Herchsaba
137. Meserut
138. Nanitva
139. Eruk-sartu
140. Arakva
141. Biratet
142. Nensklar
143. Urutar
144. Virsava
145. Akbarut
146. Melsatur
147. Ranavik

148. Ukrutvravit
149. Helvanit
150. Esklavar
151. Suvanit
152. Hekvravit
153. Karusta
154. Hespi
155. Ranastu
156. Eksahur
157. Mansarat
158. Esatur
159. Kurinar
160. Resavit
161. Elektar
162. Mensarut
163. Ravanik
164. Kavanit
165. Elsaruk
166. Menserat
167. Arukstar
168. Erektu
169. Melkor
170. Nanansaruk
171. Arakvar
172. Hirskavi
173. Blivabik
174. Urusta 1
175. Harakva
176. Kuhanit
177. Lisater
178. Gravanuk
179. Ritklaver
180. Urabik
181. Kelsatur
182. Meretur
183. Nanasit
184. Gravanik
185. Krisiter
186. Karanut

187. Sihut-ater
188. Arunasva
189. Menruk-kereta
190. Runaset
191. Hireklat
192. Marchvador
193. Nensurat
194. Rakvaplet
195. Elsavir
196. Hiresta
197. Arkplahur
198. Kerusater
199. Vibrit-klavit
200. Rasbahut
201. Kalshavit
202. Brispahur
203. Krunavach
204. Hirspahur
205. Mesbasur
206. Kiletrach
207. Esenut
208. Ereshtrave
209. Hurpahet
210. Nenklitparu
211. Hurusut
212. Esekra
213. Visebach
214. Rutpahur
215. Eleru
216. Harastu
217. Nesbarut
218. Akravit
219. Heseklut
220. Birespa
221. Mistubar
222. Rachmar
223. Blihaspat
224. Kirshbahur
225. Renesuk

226. Elsklabi
227. Isbaruk
228. Nensahur
229. Kirunat
230. Esebit
231. Suchbaver
232. Lihursat
233. Mirenech
234. Ursbanit
235. Reksavur
236. Orsenat
237. Vribavechvi
238. Stahunachvi
239. Splenunitva
240. Krinasavur
241. Urek
242. Misavech
243. Selhasunet
244. Nanserasuk
245. Elsavrik
246. Interuch
247. Harsat-manuvech
248. Tresibaru
249. Telenot
250. Karstu
251. Hereksa
252. Senechvi
253. Vrevasbaru
254. Arneksatu
255. Liseret
256. Arsanoch
257. Vrisvrabi
258. Estavik
259. Sinech-arstu
260. Sahur-manit
261. Pliset-vravi
262. Trihasanar
263. Erlalus-vravi
264. Asabak-akrich

265. Kursunas
266. Siharanus
267. Luvech-vranur
268. Selhanusabi
269. Shrechnanusat
270. Ornasat-huster
271. Prihanar-salanus
272. Sersanoch
273. Klibich-aster
274. Virserat-usunukvi
275. Gravanech
276. Kelsutar
277. Hersachvi
278. Manunechvi
279. Blishet-aranas
280. Kistrar
281. Sihuster
282. Pripravit-pretesar
283. Irinis-vaver
284. Kalanasvi
285. Aruch-balshet
286. Avrabit-suter
287. Arkmananes
288. Pliheresak
289. Hurunis
290. Mistral
291. Platplasu
292. Erkskranit
293. Urukpater
294. Kelkanish
295. Granavit
296. Erkstabit
297. Sechnunanit
298. Harasatvi-balush
299. Erebikplatur
300. Hertl-hasbavi
301. Suknet-sabavit
302. Rananek
303. Palasha

304. Nensarabruk
305. Ertl-brasbatur
306. Sunuvish-baver
307. Istrach-manut
308. Eleshner
309. Suhuvirtlbi
310. Echsabilanash
311. Brabech-huresvi
312. Gelshanadoch
313. Ursech-partpavi
314. Karanash-selhatut
315. Vilesmanunit
316. Meshpahur-akrat
317. Serchsavir
318. Kirsh-pater
319. Ritva-balanuk
320. Niskaret
321. Prekpranuhish
322. Skertlhat
323. Rinesat
324. Suhach-ornit
325. Entre-blavanish
326. Biraset
327. Kihur
328. Elsenar
329. Sutrivat
330. Eskrahu
331. Susi-anar
332. Kerstanur
333. Hilspabit
334. Truhaspava
335. Kiru-sesavit
336. Itrihat-ekla
337. Huravit
338. Kilichvar
339. Nesusklavet
340. Pitrubar
341. Isterenot
342. Utribaret

343. Karsahit
344. Erulestranet
345. Menhuvravit
346. Asvach-paret
347. Kanahis
348. Etrehus
349. Misaravet
350. Kitrubaret
351. Ananaklavi
352. Utrubaret
353. Hespa-kinuves
354. Suhuch-navet
355. Kenenut
356. Anasa-usabrit
357. Klirasut
358. Entemplehur
359. Nasahus
360. Kinahir
361. Netrebit
362. Karatu
363. Hisba
364. Nanek
365. Tra-uva
366. Sisatu
367. Eksaru
368. Klisara
369. Hekstu
370. Karanu
371. Hareksa
372. Nensara
373. Virasta
374. Husklava
375. Reneksu
376. Maravech-arana
377. Vrasaru
378. Irikta
379. Biraret
380. Nereksu
381. Balestu

382. Harakta
383. Usava
384. Neruk
385. Avara
386. Nurparet
387. Haranach
388. Rustahet
389. Ranuret
390. Vruchtaret
391. Kiranat
392. Heresatu
393. Misharu
394. Nansaru
395. Erkplata
396. Haravit
397. Rusaver
398. Kurunut
399. Ratvravir
400. Harsatu
401. Uruk-nanes
402. Helsata
403. Vibret-urusvi
404. Harchnahut
405. Sipre-urut
406. Harsta-misech
407. Ukru-varasbi
408. Hesta-misech
409. Rutvrabi
410. Hanasat
411. Ukrevi
412. Hirkpata
413. Blubech
414. Suveta
415. Asba
416. Ukreta
417. Vruvabik
418. Kirivirspata
419. Nensarahik
420. Utrebik

421. Herenit
422. Haraspa
423. Mistahur
424. Blubek
425. Setrevi
426. Nusarut
427. Karanas
428. Kuvrenot
429. Barastu
430. Heresa
431. Kachbaru
432. Nasaru
433. Kuhetpata
434. Neklit-aras
435. Viset-vabru
436. Uktarut
437. Huskel-varavas
438. Eseklet-nisar
439. Avrarut- pleseta
440. Nukbara
441. Rasatu

THE DNA ROSE

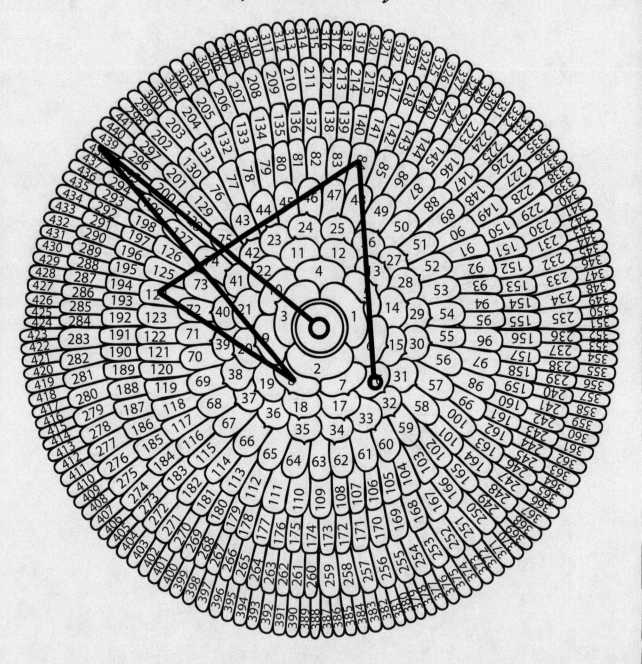

Principle of Perpetual Self-regeneration 1
Self-sustaining emotional self-sovereignty

Thirty Magical Activation
Templates for Cellular Regeneration

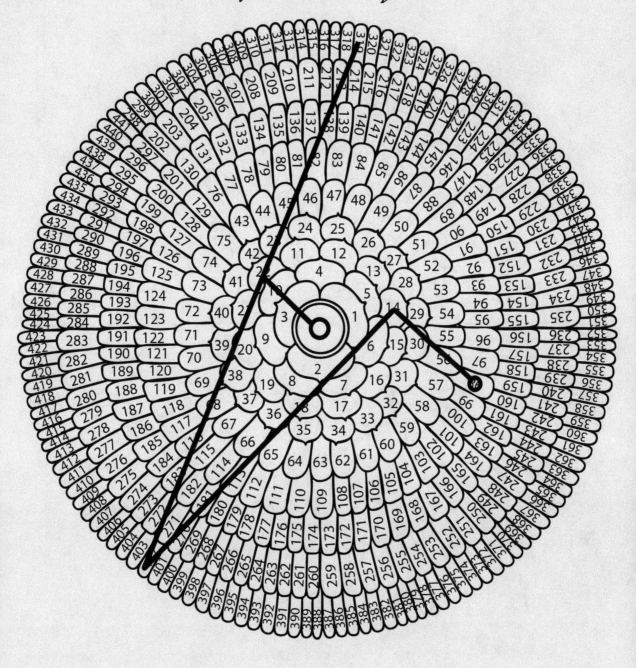

Principle of Perpetual Self-regeneration 2
Self-contained energy production

Thirty Magical Activation Templates for Cellular Regeneration

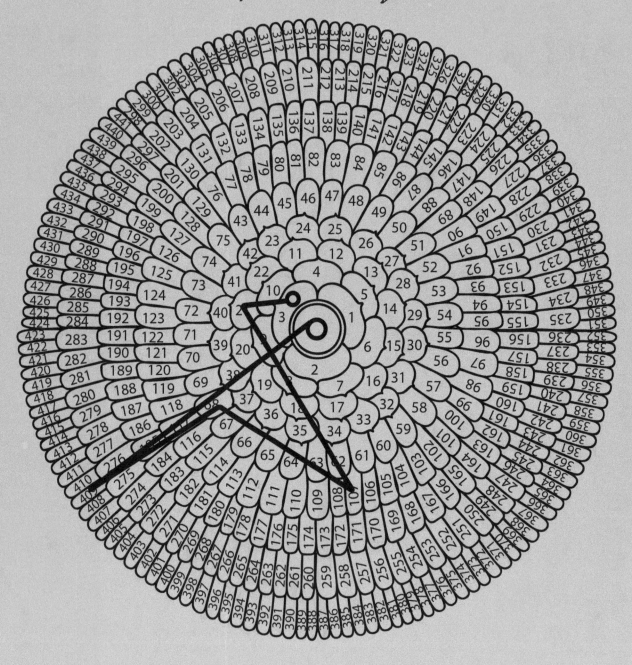

Principle of Perpetual Self-regeneration 3
Fully-used, complete pranic circuit

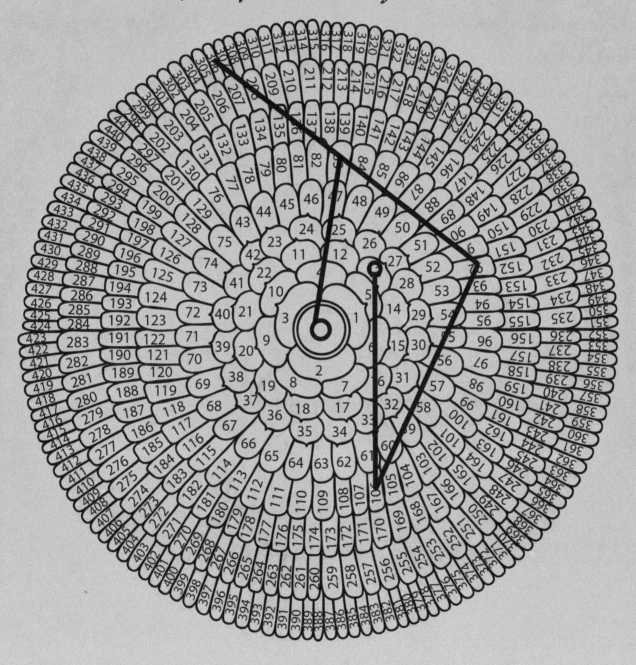

Principle of Perpetual Self-regeneration 4
Masterful directiveness within complete surrender

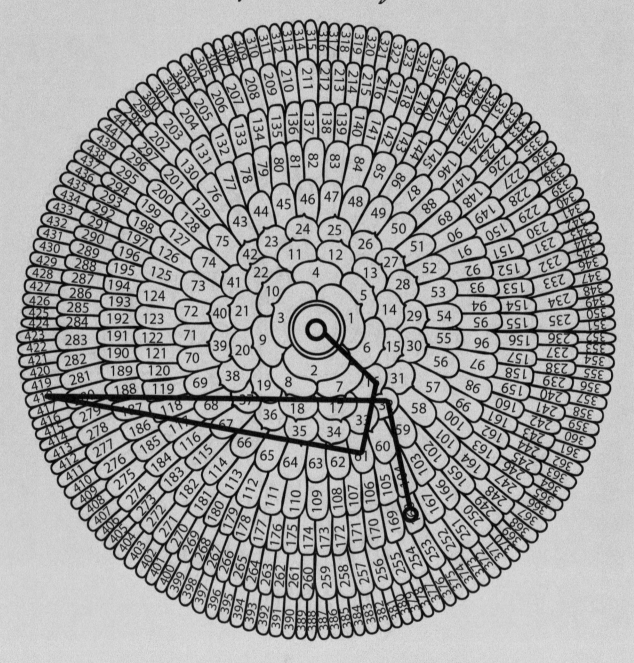

Principle of Perpetual Self-regeneration 5
Withdrawing from the games of mirrors

Thirty Magical Activation
Templates for Cellular Regeneration

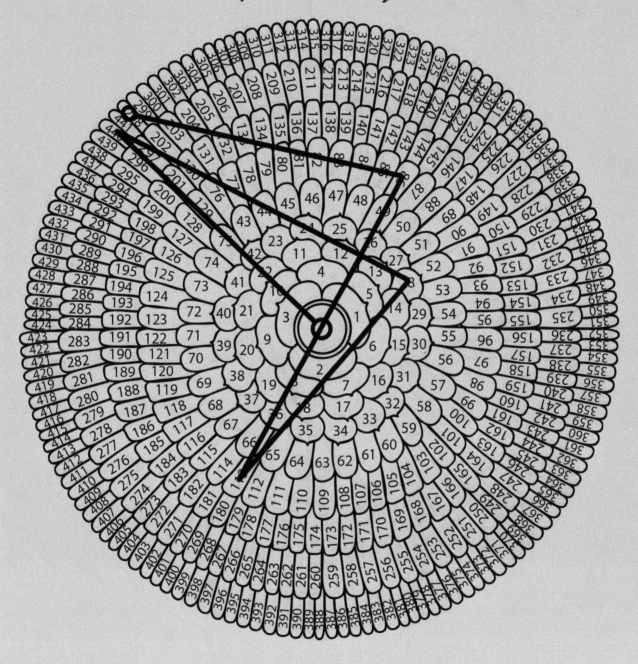

Principle of Perpetual Self-regeneration 6
Existence beyond body, soul and spirit

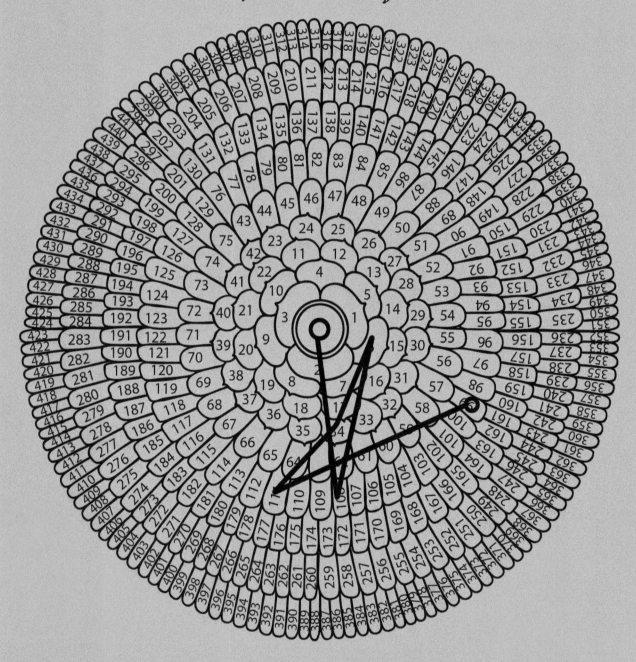

Principle of Perpetual Self-regeneration 7
Timelessness through surrender

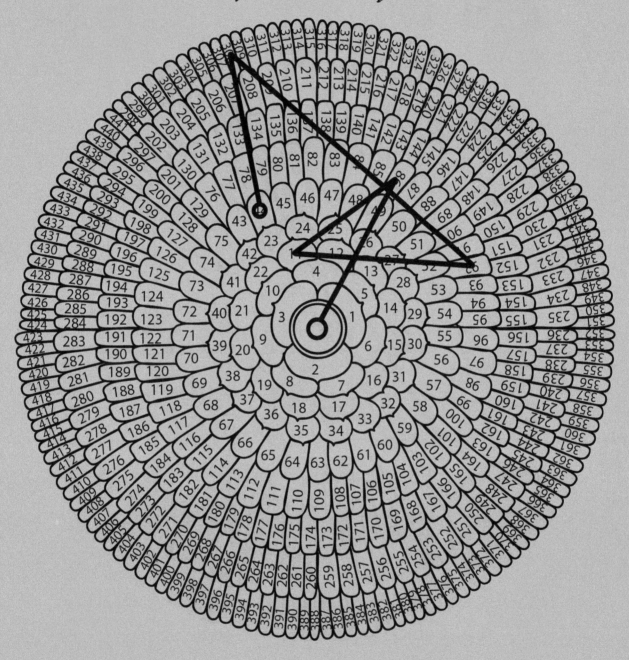

*Principle of Perpetual Self-regeneration 8
Fluid release of linear time*

319

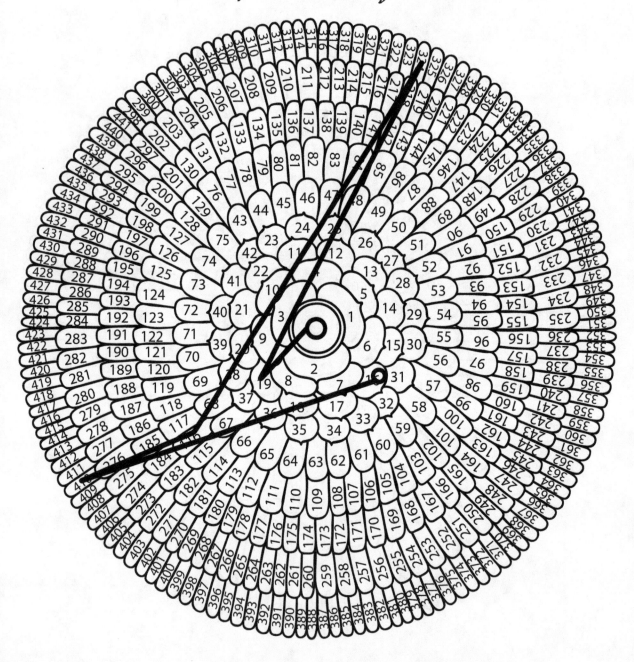

Principle of Perpetual Self-regeneration 9
Spacelessness through appreciative perspectives

Thirty Magical Activation Templates for Cellular Regeneration

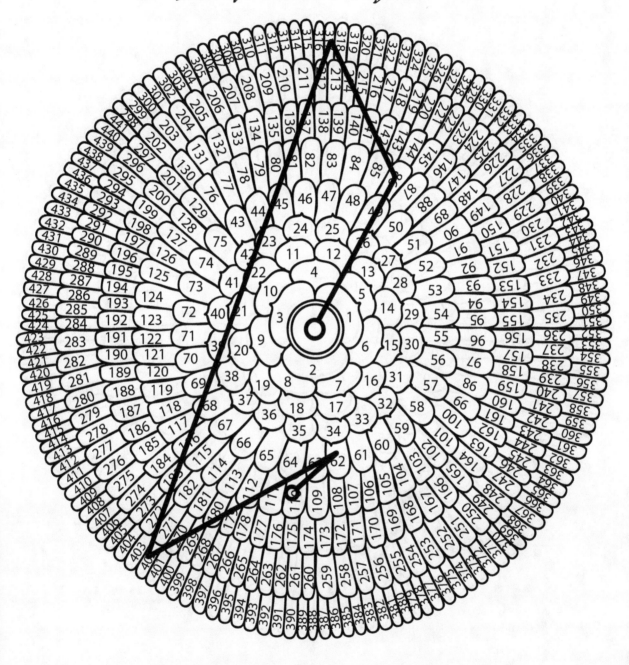

Principle of Perpetual Self-regeneration 10
Existing as the impervious source of our reality

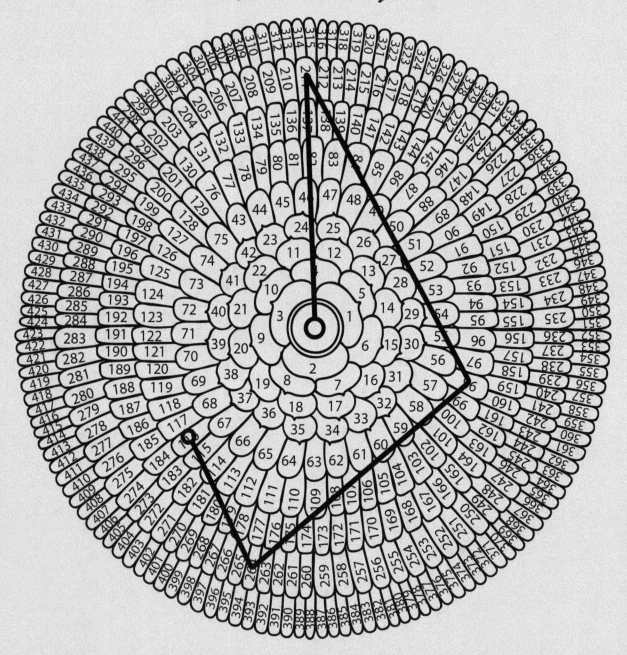

Principle of Perpetual Self-regeneration 11
Innovative dancer of the eternal song

Thirty Magical Activation
Templates for Cellular Regeneration

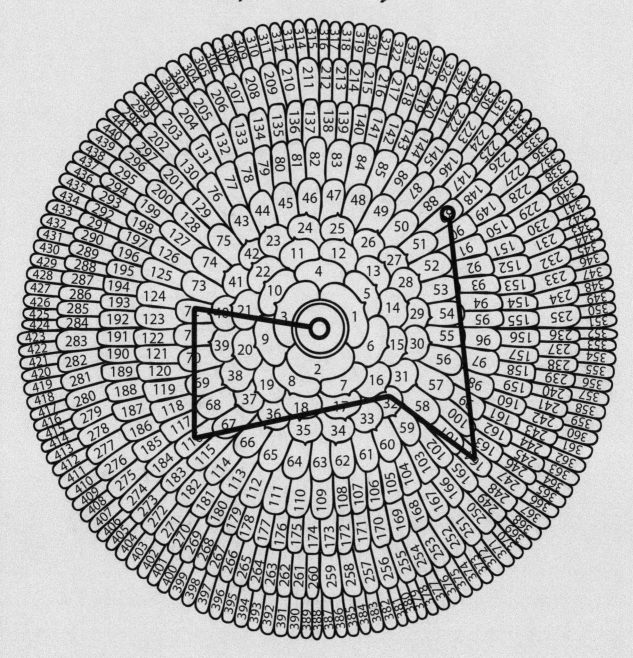

Principle of Perpetual Self-regeneration 12
Allowing the joyous shaping of our ever–renewing form

Thirty Magical Activation Templates for Cellular Regeneration

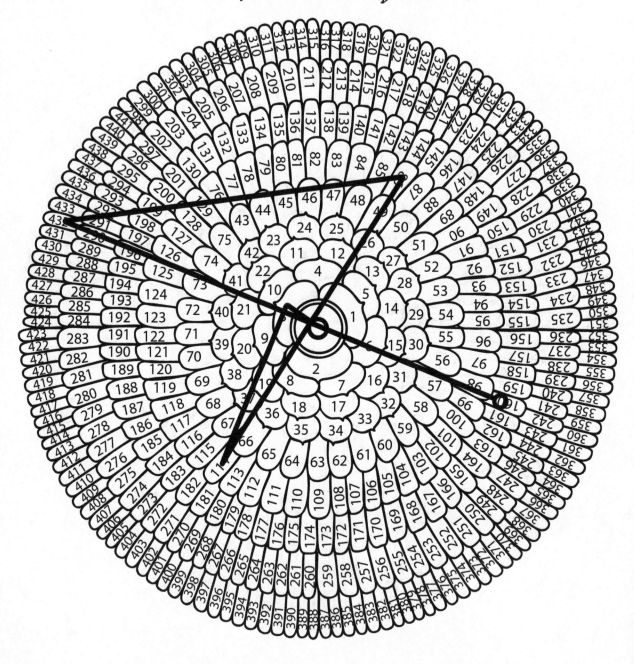

Principle of Perpetual Self-regeneration 13
Delightful miracle of expression as form

Thirty Magical Activation
Templates for Cellular Regeneration

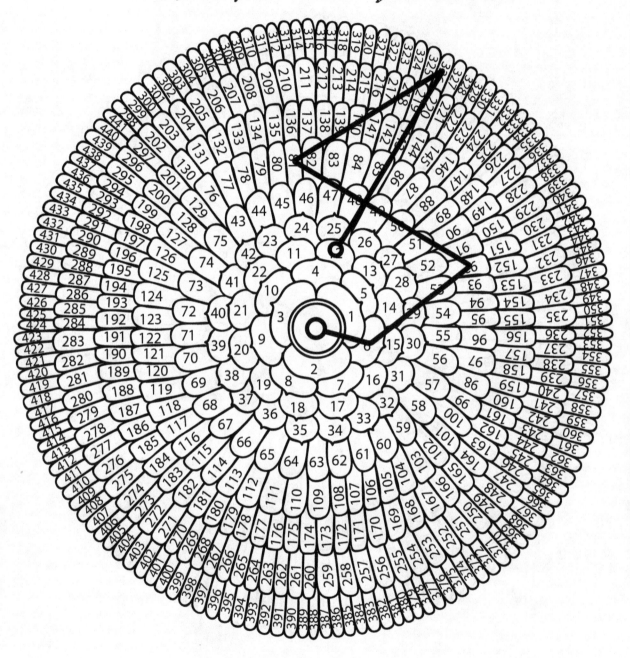

Principle of Perpetual Self-regeneration 14
Inspired enthusiasm of self-regenerating form

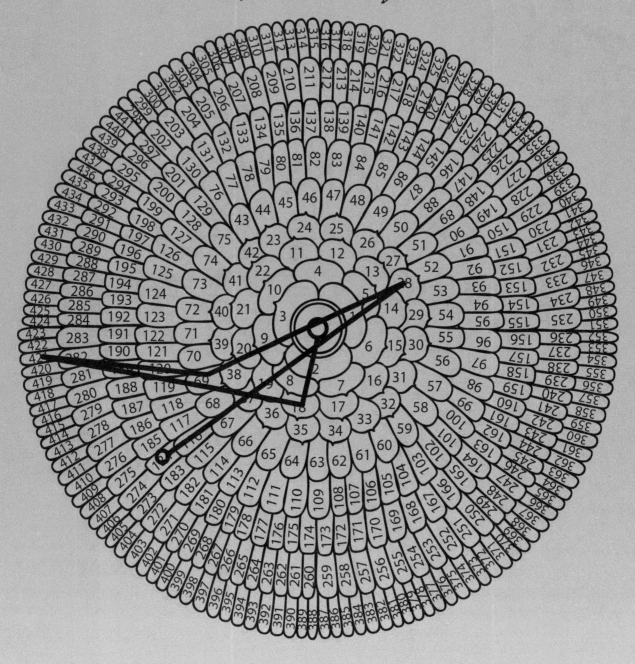

Principle of Perpetual Self-regeneration 15
Victorious expression of incorruptible matter

Thirty Magical Activation
Templates for Cellular Regeneration

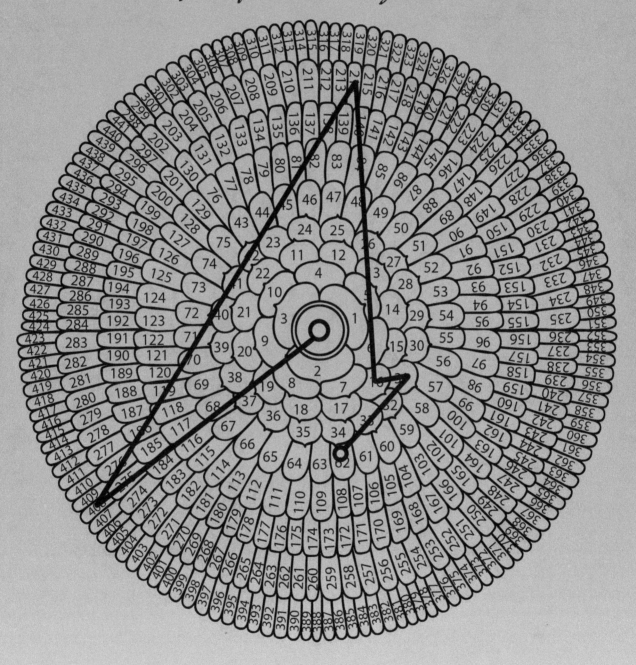

Principle of Perpetual Self-regeneration 16
Strengthened conviction of miraculous existence

327

Thirty Magical Activation
Templates for Cellular Regeneration

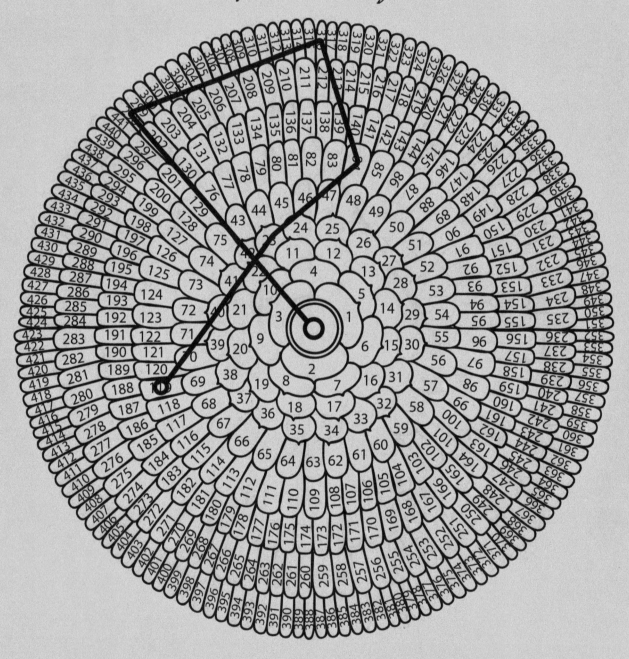

Principle of Perpetual Self-regeneration 17
Marveling at the awakened gifts of the body

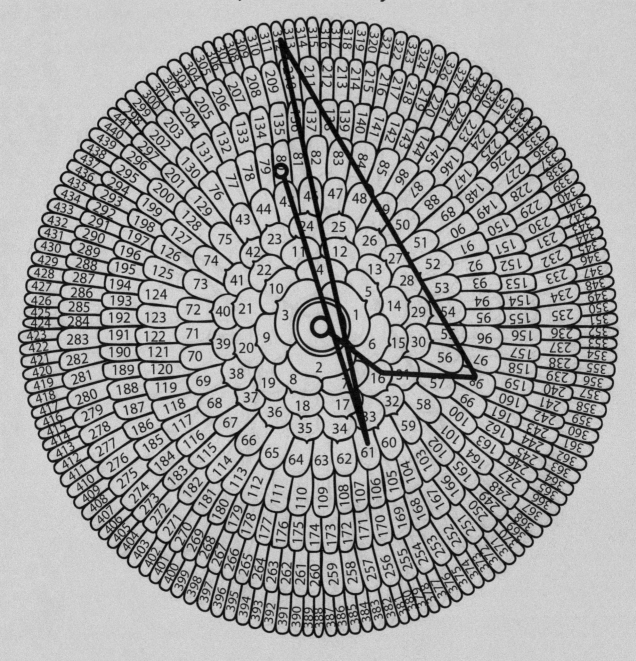

Principle of Perpetual Self-regeneration 18
Interpretive dancer of the joyous dance of Infinite expression

Thirty Magical Activation
Templates for Cellular Regeneration

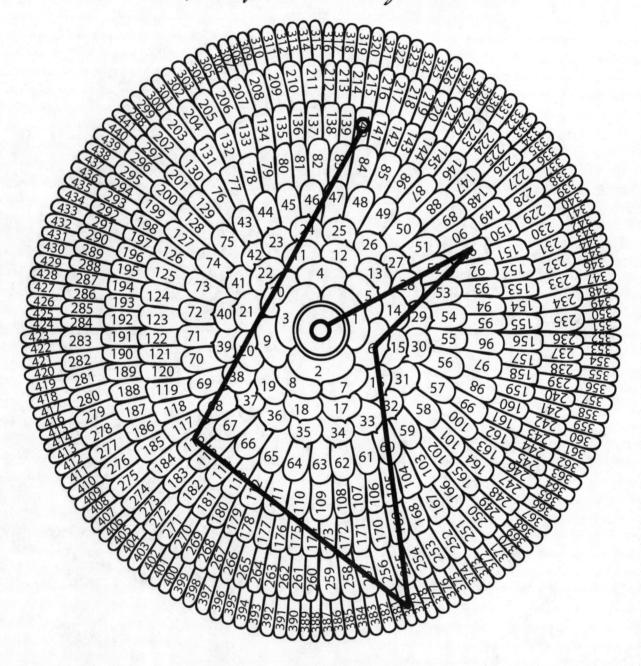

Principle of Perpetual Self-regeneration 19
The gentle guidance of the subtle currents of the ocean of Infinite existence

Thirty Magical Activation
Templates for Cellular Regeneration

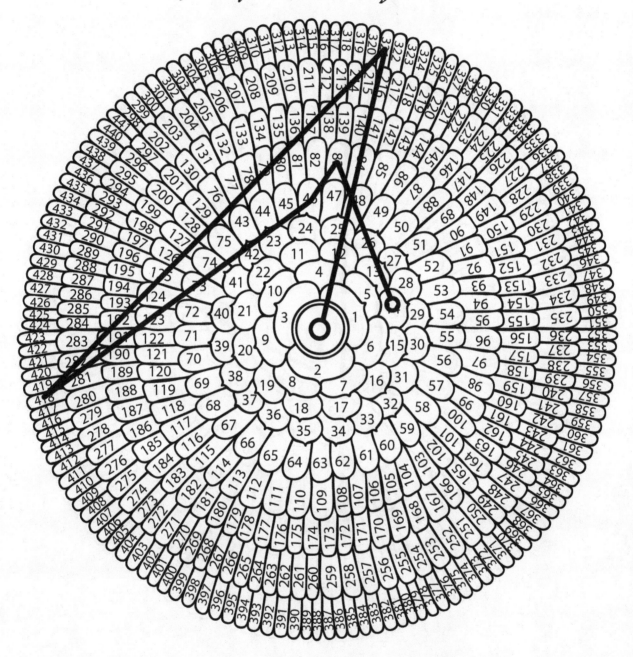

Principle of Perpetual Self-regeneration 20
Childlike wonderment and glad expectations

Thirty Magical Activation Templates for Cellular Regeneration

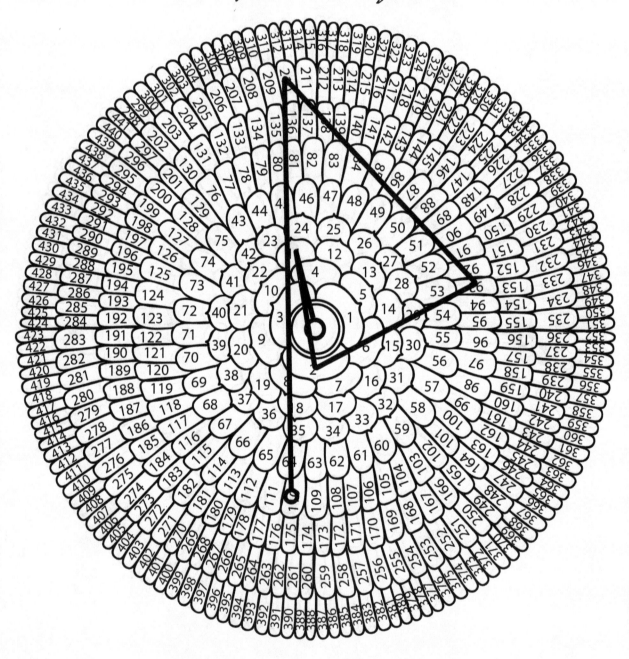

Principle of Perpetual Self-regeneration 21
Open receptivity to the unfathomable wonders of existence

Thirty Magical Activation Templates for Cellular Regeneration

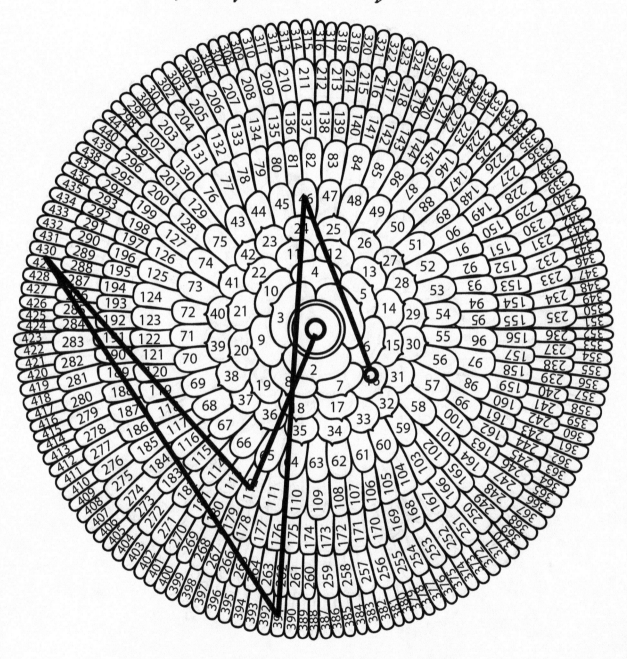

Principle of Perpetual Self-regeneration 22
The adventure of never-ending, aware self-discovery

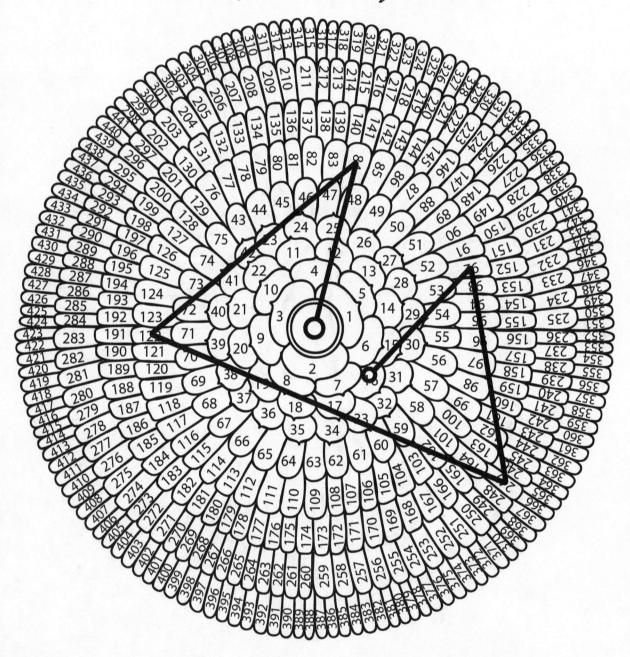

Principle of Perpetual Self-regeneration 23
Freedom from limiting expectations by readiness to be amazed

Thirty Magical Activation Templates for Cellular Regeneration

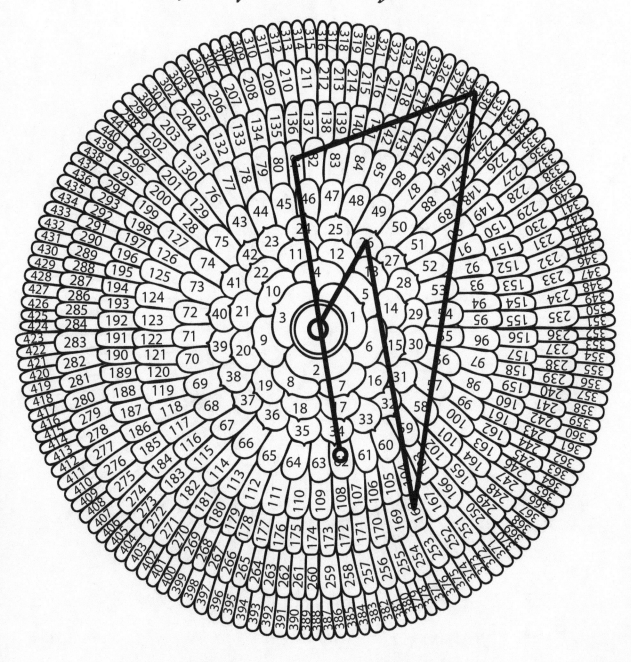

Principle of Perpetual Self-regeneration 24
Self-generated inspiration for the graceful artistry of expression

Thirty Magical Activation
Templates for Cellular Regeneration

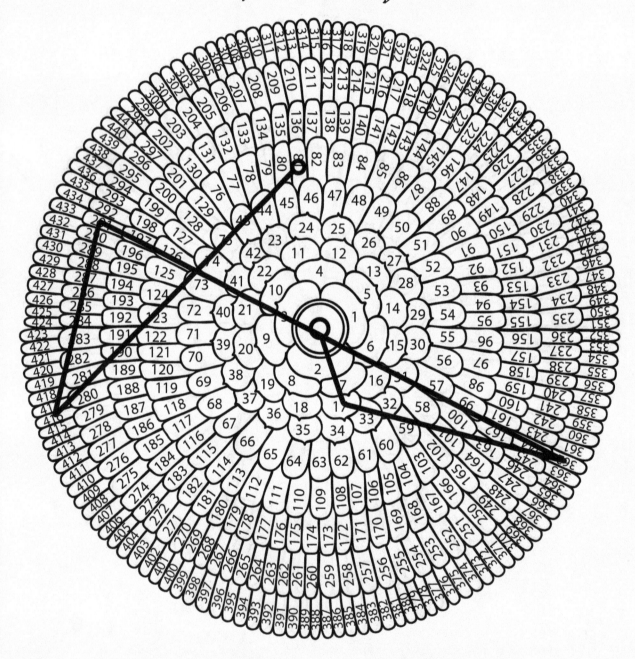

Principle of Perpetual Self-regeneration 25
Cooperation of individuality within inclusiveness

Thirty Magical Activation
Templates for Cellular Regeneration

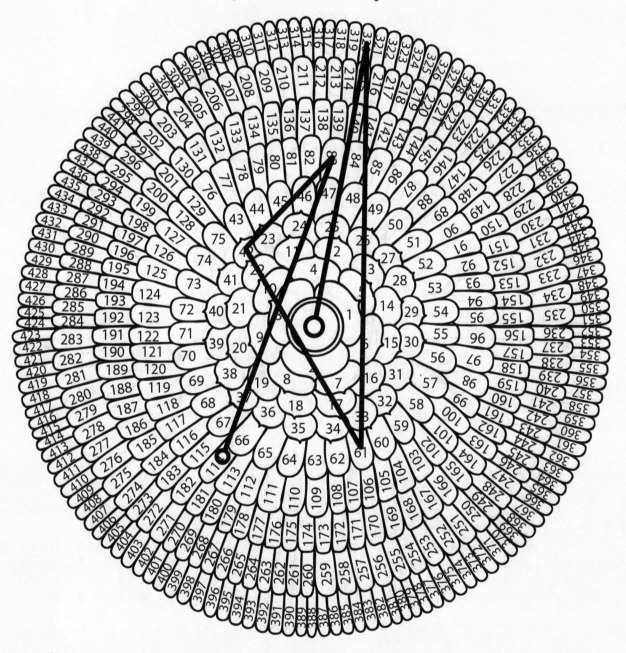

Principle of Perpetual Self-regeneration 26
Living with deliberate reverence through awareness

Thirty Magical Activation Templates for Cellular Regeneration

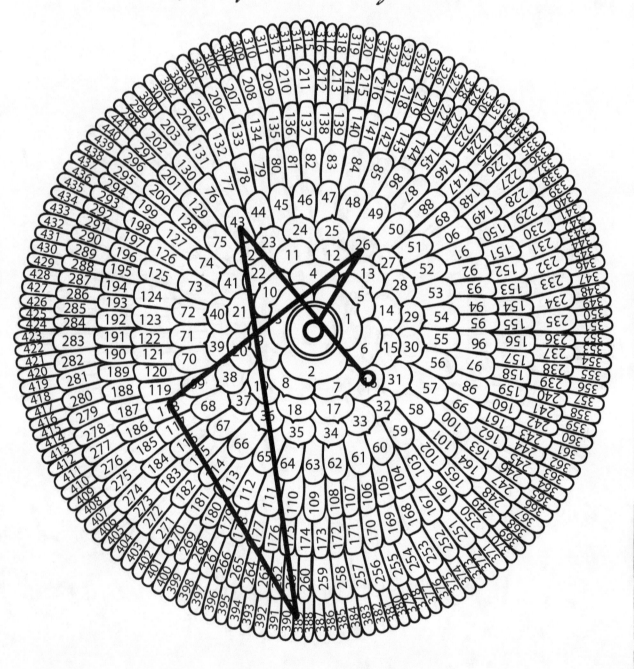

Principle of Perpetual Self-regeneration 27
Archetypal awareness of the potency of choices

338

Thirty Magical Activation
Templates for Cellular Regeneration

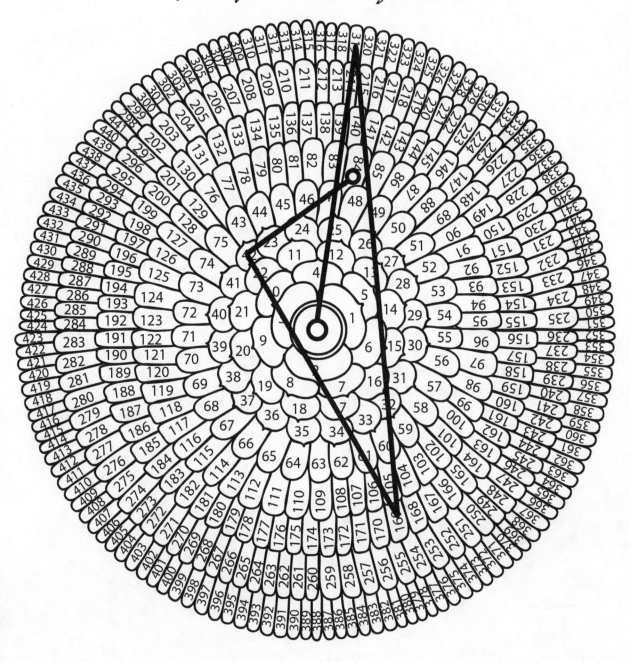

Principle of Perpetual Self-regeneration 28
Effortless movement through eternity

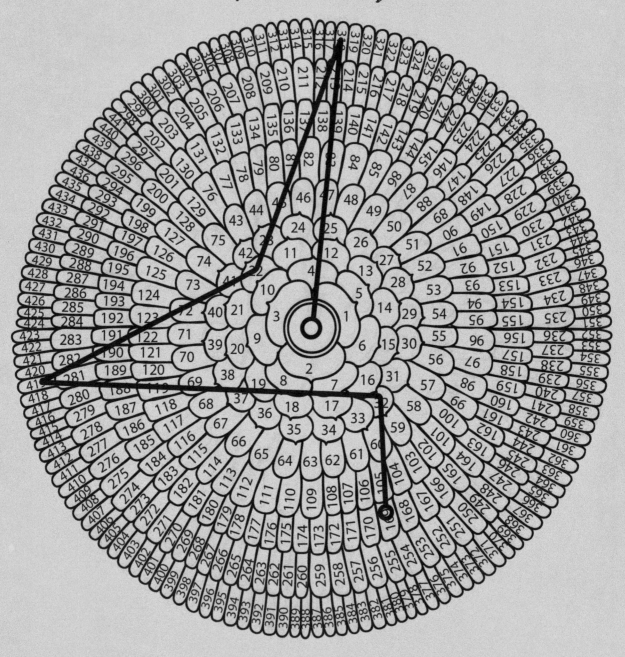

*Principle of Perpetual Self-regeneration 29
Being our own source of boundless vitality*

Thirty Magical Activation Templates for Cellular Regeneration

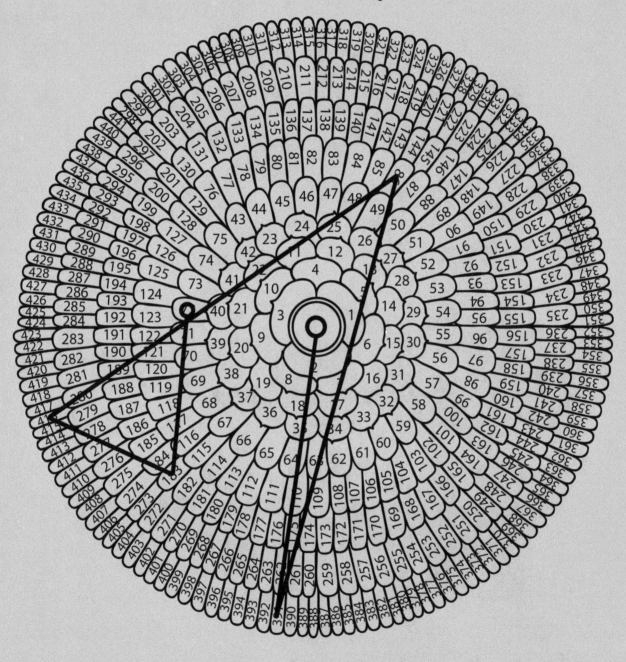

Principle of Perpetual Self-regeneration 30
Effortless miraculous achievements without end

The Shield to Safeguard the Magic of the Gods

The Book of Spells
as a Power Object
that Cancels
Black Magic

*Power Wheel
for the Book of Spells*

*Kenevech herseta uskretvi manunes herasvi
Asach nenuvi haras erseta kluvi eseret kluva*

Let the body of magic incorruptible, given
in compassion, negate that which in hostility comes

345

Closing

The Ages of Forgetfulness are coming to an end. The reclamation of the self-empowerment of humanity is at hand to awaken the inherent gifts that are his birthright. The pristine magic that once was his, must once again dawn.

To facilitate the awakening of man's incorruptible magical abilities, the Magical Kingdoms have delivered their magic after ages of secrecy. The collective body of magical information this has produced forms an alchemical equation that acts upon the reader to awaken codes in the DNA and evolve awareness.

This priceless and holy gift to humanity heralds the advent of the spiritual maturity and self-responsibility of man – the breaking of a new day of enlightenment and compassion.

Spell Finder

Book of Magic Spells, Potions and Incantations

ABUNDANCE:

BEAUTY:

BODY/PHYSICALITY:

CONCEPTION/CHILDBIRTH:

Blessing to Support Mothers-to-be - Candle 6 Secret 4, p95

To Ease Childbirth - Window 11, p231

For Attracting an Immaculate Conception - Incantation 6, p174

Immaculate Conception - Spell 3, p24

DREAMS/DESIRES:

Dream Magic - Potion for Dream Magic, p64

To Fulfill a Desire - Incantation 1, p190

To See the Future Results of Options - Incantation 4, p192

ENERGY:

Drawing Energy into a Spell - Candle 4 Secret 4, p86

Energy through Food and Clothes - Candle 3 Secret 4, p82

To Seal an Energy Drain - Window 14, p235

FAMILY:

Balance and Strength - Candle 6 Secret 2, p93

To Clear Ties with Departed Loved Ones - Giant Customs Ritual 3, p141

To Create Harmony - Window 10, p230

Family Groups - Candle 6 Secret 1, p92

The Growth of the Child - Candle 6 Secret 3, p94

Harmony - Spell 12, p33

To Keep Your Child Secure - Giant Customs Ritual 2, p138

FRIENDS:

Bring Friends - Spell 4, p42

FOOD:

Make Things 3 times Hotter - Potion for 3H Magic, p65

For Tasty Food - Giant Culture Ritual 3, p146

FUTURE/DESTINY:

Crystal (or Glass) Ball - Spell for Sacred Object 1, p122

To Enter the Hall of Destiny - Incantation 11, p204

To Get Information from the Dove Libraries - Window 7, p227

See the Future Results of Options - Incantation 4, p192

HARMONY/BALANCE:

Balance Through Color - Candle 1 Secret 2, p73

Creating an Alliance with Nature - Spell 9, p112

Fluidity - Window 6, p226

Harmony - Spell 12, p33

To Obtain Inner Balance - Incantation 9, p179

Restoration of Balance - Spell 13, p34

The Secret of Music to Balance the Emotions - Candle 1 Secret 4, p75

Stability - Spell 2, p102

HEALTH/HEALING:

To Clear the Mind - Incantation 6, p194

To Enhance Well-being - Incantation 2, p190

For Infusing Standing Waveforms - Window 4, p222

To Heal Wounds - Window 9, p229

Healing and Balancing the Spine - Working with the Dragon Affirmations, p259

Healing Cuts and Bruises - Potion for Red Magic, p55

Pull in Assistance - Spell 8, p109

Restoration of the Tones of Emotion - Candle 1 Secret 3, p74

To Seal an Energy Drain - Window 14, p235

Strengthening & Healing Broken Bones - Potion for Orange Magic, p58

HEAT/COLD:

To Keep You Warm - Giant Culture Ritual 2, p145

Make Things 3 Times Hotter - Potion for 3H Magic, p65

INNOCENCE:

To Shield Innocence - Incantation 8, p178

MANIFESTING:

MUSIC:

NATURE:

NEGATIVITY:

To Remove Negative Emotions or Negativity from Others - Incantation 4, p173

To Undo Ill Intent - Incantation 7, p177

PLANTS:

Assistance in Growing Plants - Candle 2 Secret 3, p78

Grow Flowers and Plants - Spell 5, p26

Grow New Species of Flowers and Plants - Spell 6, p27

To Grow Seeds - Giant Culture Ritual 1, p144

Grow Seeds - Spell 8, p45

Healing Nature - Potion for Green Magic, p54

PLAY:

Balance Through Play - The Secrets of Play - Candle 2 Secret 1, p76

Helping Children Read Well - The Secret of Play - Candle 2 Secret 4, p79

POWER:

To Boost Personal Power - Incantation 8, p196

To Find Your Sigil - Giant Magic Ritual 3, p152

Increased Personal Power - Spell 3, p103

The Book of Spells as a Power Object that Cancels Black Magic, p344

PROSPERITY/OPPORTUNITY:

Abundant Prosperity - Spell 1, p101

To Accumulate Wealth - Incantation 7, p195

Opportunity - Window 3, p221

Prosperity - Window 1, p218

Pull in Assistance - Spell 8, p109

PROTECTION:

To Keep Your Child Secure - Giant Customs Ritual 2, p138

Protect a Child - Spell 9, p46

REMEMBERING:

For Remembering - Potion for Yellow Magic, p57

To Remember Past Lives - Incantation 6, p186

TELEPATHY/ESP:

To Communicate with the Spirit World - Ritual 3, p212

To Cultivate Telepathy - Incantation 2, p184

To Increase the Accuracy of Divination - Incantation 3, p185

For Remote Viewing - Incantation 5, p186

TRAVEL:

Embarkation - Window 2, p219

TRUTH:

To Discern the Truth - Potion for Red Hand Magic, p68

Discern the Truth of Another - Spell 10, p46

For Truth to Be Revealed - Incantation 3, p172

Freedom from Illusion - Spell 10, p31

To Solve a Mystery - Incantation 2, p172

Stability - Spell 2, p102

The Sword of Discernment - Spell 4, p104

WATER:

Cleansing or Increasing the Supply of Water - Potion for Blue Magic, p56

WORK/TASKS:

To Evoke Twenty-four Lords of Light - Window 12, p232

Pull in Assistance - Spell 8, p109

The Secrets of Work - Balance - Candle 3 Secret 1, p80

The Secrets of Work - Fueled by Joy - Candle 3 Secret 2, p81

Success - Candle 3 Secret 3, p82

YOUTH:

To Balance Gravitation with Levitation - Ritual 2, p211

To Create the Fountain of Youth - Ritual 1, p210

Return of Youth - Spell 2, p23

To Reverse the Signs of Aging - Window 8, p228

Printed in the USA
CPSIA information can be obtained
at www.ICGtesting.com
LVHW071238251123
764421LV00076B/768